THE
INJURED HORSE

Hands-on Methods for Managing and Treating Injuries

AMANDA SUTTON

David & Charles

DEDICATION

To all those who have shared and helped to disseminate their knowledge to me.

ACKNOWLEDGEMENTS

There are so many people who have helped in this book's compilation, I have been so fortunate to have such support from all at my practice and from all my professional colleagues.

Thank you also to all staff at David & Charles; without their help and tolerance this book would not have been possible.

Foreword by William Fox-Pitt

The perfect physical horse does not exist and like any human athlete, competition horses need maintenance to keep them in top condition.

Physiotherapy, including massage, osteopathy and acupuncture, plays a significant role in the production of an equine athlete. Several of my horses have had their career spans lengthened thanks to an ongoing programme of treatment. A good example is Stunning, whose career began on the track in New Zealand as a two-year-old. It was inevitable that, by the time he came to me at 13, he showed a fair amount of wear and tear. He was 17 in 2003 and due to regular physiotherapy treatment he has competed in 18 three-day events, never having needed time off.

Nevertheless most competition horses incur injury at some stage during their careers. Close veterinary monitoring combined with physiotherapy and a careful training schedule can go a long way in helping to prevent injuries, but when problems do occur the horse's rehabilitation is crucial. Giving a damaged horse time to heal is critical and during this period the correct choice of therapy can make all the difference to a rapid and full recovery.

I have no doubt that physiotherapy should be a central part in the routine of a competition horse, not only to maximise performance but, as this book shows, to promote the healthy healing of the injured horse.

During my involvement with Amanda over the last eight years I have, in witnessing the amazing results she has achieved with my horses, realised what a gift she has, and I feel most fortunate to have her as a valuable member of my team.

A DAVID & CHARLES BOOK

First published in the UK in 2003

Copyright © Amanda Sutton 2003

Distributed in North America
by F&W Publications, Inc.
4700 East Galbraith Road
Cincinnati, OH 45236
1-800-289-0963

A catalogue record for this book is available from the British Library.

ISBN 0 7153 1421 1

Printed in China by Leefung-Asco Printers Ltd.
for David & Charles
Brunel House   Newton Abbot   Devon

Commissioning Editor: Jane Trollope
Desk Editor: Shona Wallis
Art Editor: Sue Cleave
Project Editor: Anne Plume
Production: Ros Napper

Visit our website at www.davidandcharles.co.uk

David & Charles books are available from all good bookshops; alternatively you can contact our Orderline on (0)1626 334555 or write to us at FREEPOST EX2110, David & Charles Direct, Newton Abbot, TQ12 4ZZ (no stamp required UK mainland).

Glossary of terms

(see also individual sections)

abduction	moving a limb away from the body
acute	a recent injury
adduction	moving a limb towards the body
adhesion	fibrous band causing restriction in the tissue
anterior	situated at the front
atrophy	decreased muscle bulk due to degeneration of cells
bilateral	both sides
chronic	old problem/long-term problem
congenital	exists at birth but not necessarily hereditary
distal	further away from the centre of the body than another point of reference
dorsal	the back or more towards the back than another point of reference
endorphins	the body's natural pain-killing chemicals
extension	the straightening of a limb
flexion	bending
fossa	a hollow
hyperaemia	enhanced circulation
hypertrophy	overdevelopment of muscle
insertion	point of attachment of muscle to bone that is further from the centre of the body
ischaemia	inadequate blood flow due to pressure/constriction
lateral	position on the outer surface
medial	position on the inside surface
oedema	excess accumulation of fluid
origin	point of attachment of muscle that is closer to the centre of the body
palpation	feeling with your hands
posterior	situated at the back
prognosis	prospect of recovery
protraction	forward movement
proximal	closer to the body than another point of reference
retraction	backward movement
spasm	an involuntary contraction of muscle
ventral	the underside or more towards the underside than another point of reference

Contents

Introduction

Free grazing allows horses natural mobility as in the natural world in which they evolved

All injuries heal eventually, but not always in the most functional way. Before horses were domesticated they roamed the plains, and if they were injured they had to keep moving or else they were killed by a predator. The injury would heal, but not necessarily with the best cosmetic result.

Today we ask the horse to carry or pull weight, to travel at different speeds, on varying surfaces, and to assume postures that are often unnatural to him. If he suffers injury, treatment is selected to assist the correct healing of tissues, and the ultimate objective is that this should be with the most flexibility and strength possible. With this in mind, it is important to be able to detect even the subtlest change in tone in the soft

tissues, also to pick up on any change in the horse's posture or way of going that he might adopt in order to compensate for a weakened, injured structure: this should be monitored in order to prevent progression to irreversible damage or a chronic pain and behavioural status. This effectively means early screening and regular prophylactic care. Some injuries are obvious – there is blood, tissue damage and lameness – but there are incidents where the horse has maybe fallen, or pulled back on his halter, and although he appears to be okay in that there are no broken tissues or bones, you might well ask yourself how an animal the size of a horse can fall, perhaps twisting his frame, or crash into something, without overstretching or compressing the soft tissue and axial skeleton.

This book explains the cycle of events that

takes place when a horse injures himself. First it describes the physical changes that occur in the horse's body as it organises itself to cope with the damage and set the healing process in motion. For the veterinarian and horse owner, sometimes identifying the exact seat of injury is a problem, so this is considered, as are the methods of diagnosis. Then the three main ways of treating injury are discussed, namely cold therapy, the propitious application of heat, and finally electrotherapy. And just as important and crucial as the treatment administered is the nursing and aftercare the horse receives, to restore him to his full capabilities.

All these aspects of diagnosis, treatment and aftercare are fully investigated, so your horse will have the best chance of being restored to his full athletic ability.

Left and below: Sustaining this amount of compression through the body can cause long-term mobility problems

Injury and its Immediate Effects

So what actually happens when an injury occurs? First, damage to the tissues immediately sets up inflammation, a process in which lymph is produced, whose purpose is to fill the interstices in the tissues caused by the injury. This results in swelling and pain, so the horse rests the affected area; nevertheless it is the beginning of healing, because the lymph encourages the formation of repair tissue, or scar tissue. This process must be controlled and manipulated, however, otherwise the scar tissue will be laid down in haphazard fashion – not in alignment with the part it relates to – resulting in the horse ending up with possibly less mobility than if the repair process had been actively managed.

The Inflammatory Process

GLOSSARY OF TERMS

Platelets: Disc-shaped cell structures present in the blood, used by the body to arrest bleeding.

Coagulation: The forming of a blood clot.

Phagocytes: Cells which destroy microorganisms, other cells and foreign particles, such as white blood cells.

Exudate: Proteins and white blood cells which pass through the walls of intact blood vessels, as a result of inflammation. Exudation is a normal part of the body's defence mechanism.

Interstice: A small space in a tissue or between parts of the body.

The inflammatory process begins with tissue injury, and encompasses the body's innate reactions to such damage. Both the immune and blood-clotting systems are alerted, and an interrelated sequence of events ensues, driven on by a mixture of chemical and cellular factors.

The major series of events immediately following tissue wounding are a result of blood- and lymph-vessel disruption, consequently the leaking of blood constituents, the reorganisation of platelets, and ultimately blood coagulation. The purpose of these events is to provide a cleansing service in the area, in the form of phagocytic cells that engulf bacteria and other cellular debris and so guard the system against infection. Once this is performed, the sequential repair mechanisms can proceed normally. Occasionally the latter process is not totally efficient, and a state known as chronic inflammation ensues. The acute inflammatory stage usually lasts only 1–3 days, and overlaps with the next phase.

Thus injury acts as an irritant and produces inflammation, and the effects of this can spread to a great distance from the seat of the original injury. This inflammation is nature's preliminary process towards repair, as it produces just what is required, namely a heightened blood and lymph supply, to effect that repair. As the exudate forces itself into the interstices of the tissues, the tissues become stretched so causing pain, and according to the degree of pain the animal rests the part, but only through the actual range of movement which is painful, provided he is allowed to move.

The object of the oozing lymph is to fill the space caused by the injury and join up the parted structures. The final result is an almost non-vascular, tough, non-elastic fibrous scar tissue. All would be well if this scar tissue formed only between the ends of the structures torn by the injury, but unless it is controlled – by cold therapy, heat therapy, electrotherapy, and so on – this new scar tissue forms wherever the exudate reaches, forming non-elastic, tough fibrous tissue called adhesions.

During inflammation muscles function less well because they are restricted with exuded matter, and the nutrition of the muscles by fresh blood is reduced. In chronic inflammation there is less heat, but the swelling is persistent and the formation of new adhesive tissue abundant. Inflammation may be Nature's remedy in the

Lymphangitis caused by an injury to the fetlock

Effects of oozing lymph and the resulting adhesions

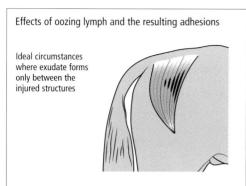

Ideal circumstances where exudate forms only between the injured structures

What actually happens. The exudate forms between the ends of the torn tissues and it spreads between the surrounding structures. If not controlled it will form adhesions and scar tissue.

natural state, but in the artificial state in which horses are kept, it requires guiding and controlling if the best recoveries are to be obtained.

CONTROLLING ADHESIONS

In the early stages these adherent surfaces are easily drawn apart; later they become stronger, in fact so strong that movement is impossible. Adhesions may form in any part of the body, but especially so in the synovial linings of joints, tendon sheaths and the connective tissue, so abundant in muscles and in ligaments.

Pain, which precedes and accompanies the formation of adhesions, aids and abets the evil process because it encourages the animal to keep the part still, while movement would in fact prevent the sticking process. From this it is obvious that to force an inflamed part to be kept an unduly long time at rest is only to assist this adhesive process. Properly controlled movements must be started before it is too late.

STRAINS AND SPRAINS

The word 'strain' is used to denote injury to muscle alone, and 'sprain' to define injury to the structures of a joint and to its muscles. It should be noted that injured muscle leads to joint stress and therefore predisposes it to injury, and they are therefore both connected.

If the strain is only slight, no actual damage is sustained by the muscle tissue, but it loses its tone and its ability to contract. It thus loses its alertness to contract to a sudden stress and so is unable to protect fully the joint it works. Some of the muscle fibres may be slightly torn, and the delicate connective tissue injured. Stretching of the affected area causes discomfort.

In severe strain, muscle tissue is actually torn and also the connective tissue. The lymphatic tissues with which this tissue is so well supplied are ruptured, and coagulable lymph is poured into the surrounding tissues, causing pain. There will be a considerable amount of blood freed from the ruptured blood vessels.

The animal tries to obtain relief by holding the part still, and in a position whereby the injured tissues have the least strain. As there is no movement, absorption of the escaped fluids is delayed and their stagnation follows. Adhesions form, further restricting movement. The animal continues to rest the part, and so the adhesions become stronger, with resultant muscle atrophy.

Pain

PAIN MODULATION

One of the main aims of treatment by all the approaches in this book is to provide pain relief.

CYCLE OF PAIN PRODUCTION

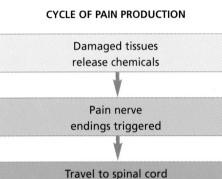

Damaged tissues release chemicals

↓

Pain nerve endings triggered

↓

Travel to spinal cord

↓

Then to cerebral cortex where pain is perceived

↓

Here pain is modulated

In the early stages of tissue trauma, we attempt to affect the circulatory response. This is usually in the form of cold therapy, which brings about a reduction in pain.

EFFECTS OF COLD ON CIRCULATION AND PAIN

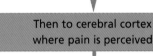

Ice

↓

Circulation affected

↓

Removal of chemicals from the area

↓

Reduces the level of pain nerve endings being triggered

PAIN RELIEF USING ELECTROTHERAPY

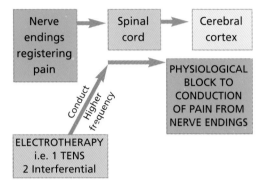

In 1965 Melzack and Wall postulated the theory of the 'pain gate'.

THE PAIN GATE

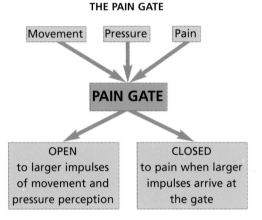

Movement   Pressure   Pain

PAIN GATE

OPEN to larger impulses of movement and pressure perception

CLOSED to pain when larger impulses arrive at the gate

Many physiotherapeutic agents and complementary therapies cause stimulation of these larger diameter nerves. Therefore the use of manipulation, TENS, heat, ice, massage, vibration and movement can produce a reduction of pain by 'closing the pain gate'.

SUMMARY

Thus it can be appreciated that if the horse is to regain full motility in the injured part, the healing process must be actively managed by the veterinarian and/or horse keeper.

The Body's Response to Injury

The body's response to soft tissue damage is quite predictable, and there are several ways in which the veterinarian and/or horse keeper can manage and influence the physical changes that ensue. Inevitably soft tissue injury involves the rupture of the associated blood vessels, which in fact initiates a healing response.

Healing progresses in basically three main phases, beginning with that of inflammation: this involves the production of lymph, causing swelling, and the laying down of scar tissue. As we shall see, controlling inflammation – by means of heat, cold, electrotherapy and controlled exercise – is important if the horse is to resume his full capability. Second is the regeneration phase, beginning at about the fifth day after the injury; treatment can be considered as having seven objectives, and is basically to restore strength and fitness.

The third phase involves the remodelling of connective tissue, where the seven objectives in treatment are the same, but the therapies are more demanding because the overall aim is to restore the horse's status quo.

Phase 1: Inflammation

GLOSSARY OF TERMS
Collagen: An inert substance, the main protein of skin, tendon, bone, cartilage and connective tissue.
Haemorrhagic phase: The first 24–48hr post injury.
Lag phase: 48hr–5 days post injury.

The inflammatory reaction involves cellular changes and swelling, producing an increased diffusion of blood vessels, and so an accumulation of white blood cells that contribute to the healing process.

WHAT HAPPENS?

In the 24–72 hours post injury, the cells that make up fibrous tissue proliferate and progressively change in character to give greater tensile strength. In the first twelve hours, granulation tissue (proud flesh) cells need oxygen and nutrition. To achieve this, the cells surrounding the injured capillaries divide, and over the next three days cell division continues, and solid capillary buds are formed. These grow towards the areas where the concentration of oxygen is low, and so the blood supply begins to approach the injured area.

The cells of the capillary walls begin to grow from 12–24 hours post injury, and there is similar change in nearby fibrous tissue cells (fibrocytes). These are normally thin and dormant, but begin to fatten up and move towards the injured area. By day five, fibrils of collagen are laid down; vitamin C is particularly important at this stage. The fibrils

multiply and become bundles of collagen, so forming the characteristic fibrous tissue of repair in a healing injury. Less fortunate is the fact that the collagen gradually shortens once formed, and contraction continues from three weeks to six months. Furthermore, new scar tissue will always shorten *unless* it is repeatedly stretched. However, fibrous healing is stronger if natural movement is encouraged: this causes the collagen to rotate to a position relevant to the directional pull on the tissue exerted during exercise, and so increases the strength of the tissue.

WHAT TO DO?

As we have seen, gentle exercise provides natural tensions in the healing tissue, and the resulting new tissue is much stronger. Healing requires a good blood supply to carry oxygen and nutrients to the worker cells; equally, repair is hindered by a poor blood supply.

Therefore the aims of treatment during the lag phase (48hr–5 days after the injury) are to:

- minimise the initial haemorrhage;
- control swelling;
- prevent tension from being applied to the primary site of tissue damage;
- help control the inflammatory reaction by dealing with the complication of the trauma, and by creating the correct environment for healing.

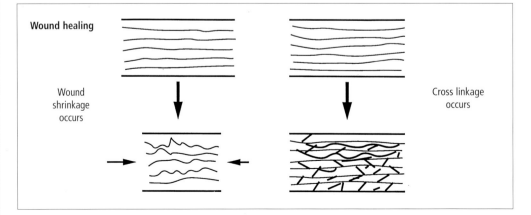

Wound healing

Wound shrinkage occurs

Cross linkage occurs

TREATMENT

The methods used for achieving these aims can be summarised as R.I.C.E.:

> **R(est).I(ce).C(ompression).E(levation).**

Rest

This will vary from controlled movement to immobilisation. In the first 24–48 hours post injury, total immobilisation of the affected area is advisable to limit haemorrhage and control swelling. In fact during this period it is also important that the patient rests in general, since activity at this time would increase cardiac output, and therefore increase the blood flow to the affected area and so increase haemorrhage from the wound.

After 48 hours, controlled movement may be allowed, but it must not be painful for the horse, and it must not tension the affected area. It is recommended that tension should not be applied to a wound before day five, because the clotting process would still be so vulnerable.

Though rest is important in the early stages post injury (24–48hr approx), beyond this period it has limited value in the treatment of soft tissue injury. With just a few specific exceptions – for example, stress fractures – complete rest of the affected area is detrimental to the healing

process; rather, careful, graduated motion applied to the affected area is essential to promote the increase in tissue tensile strength discussed above.

Ice

It is believed that the application of ice to the affected area will:

- diminish the inflammatory reaction;
- reduce swelling;
- reduce haemorrhage;
- act as an analgesic.

It also appears that the effects of ice can be maximised by the inclusion of compression during and following the period of ice application. This type of treatment is most effective if applied immediately after ice therapy; it declines over a 30-minute period.

The time of application recommended for ice varies. In the first 24–48 hours, 10 minutes is suggested to avoid the 'Hunting Lewis' reaction: this is a reversal of the constriction of blood vessels to a dilation effect, which would result in more bleeding.

> **KEY POINT:** Always protect the skin when applying ice: examine before, during and after application, and use a wet towel or 'tubigrip' in between ice and skin.

Applying ice in an acute situation

Do not apply a commerical ice pack direct to the skin, it can cause skin burns

15

The use of a Flowtron pump is one method of applying compression to an injured limb

Compression

Compression has the effect of helping to disperse the fluids involved in swelling.

It can be applied in the following ways:

- manually – by massage;
- mechanically, for instance 'Flowtron';
- bandage and tape.

KEY POINT: In the first 24–48 hours post injury compression is usually applied in a way that combines compression and limitation of motion to enforce rest. After 24–48 hours the compression is still maintained but movement may be allowed, but without tensioning the affected area. Ice and compression combined give the most effective way of reducing swelling.

Elevation

Although in most cases it is difficult to elevate the affected part, if it can be achieved it undoubtedly helps with lymphatic drainage. The key rule is to have the affected area higher than the heart.

KEY POINT: Elevation is usually combined with other adjuncts that increase lymphatic drainage, for instance gentle, pain-free, range-of-motion exercises (though these should not be attempted in the first 24–48 hours post injury), compression or massage. The lymphatic vessels have valves, and such range-of-motion exercise, combined with compression, produces a gentle milking action that may increase lymphatic flow by up fifteen times the resting level.

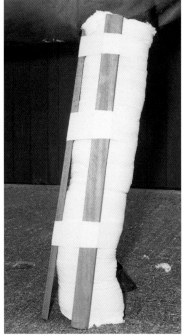

Using a Robert Jones bandage to support the foreleg. Splints can be added (left) to immobilise the limb

Passive movements stimulate the horse's circulation

Other Treatments

Other treatments that might be used during the lag phase are:

- non-steroidal anti-inflammatory medication (NSAIDs);
- exercise;
- electrotherapy.

KEY POINT: NSAIDs are most effective when given immediately post injury. They have their maximal effect over a period of three to ten days, although in some cases they may be required for a longer period.

Non-steroidal anti-inflammatory medication: Most horses with some soft tissue lesions will be prescribed NSAIDs – the most commonly used drug in the management of soft tissue injury – and therefore it is important to be aware of their actions and side effects. In the body's reaction to injury, prostaglandins – a natural hormone-like substance – are central to the inflammatory response because they help initiate a healing blood supply. However, the initial inflammatory reaction is usually much greater than what is required to promote adequate healing, so to help reduce its magnitude, NSAIDs are given because of their antiprostaglandin effect.

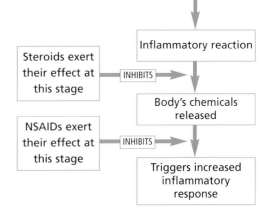

Exercise during the lag phase: Whether it be localised to the area of the lesion, or for cardiovascular fitness, exercise should not be encouraged during the stage of haemorrhage, which occurs for approximately 24–48 hours post injury. Exercise during this time period will only increase the degree of bleeding/oedema, and thus will prolong the recovery period. Once the risk of further haemorrhage has decreased, however, exercise can begin. The rationale and methods are as follows:

17

METHOD	RATIONALE

Isometric exercise
  1. Muscle stimulation
  2. Pick up opposite leg
	Given to maintain/prevent atrophy of affected muscles. Must be pain free. Used as no joint movement occurs and therefore the injured tissue (if a ligament) is not put under tension. If a muscular lesion (strain), use only when pain free.

Dynamic exercise 1. Walking in hand	Given to maintain/prevent atrophy of affected muscles. Must be pain free. The exercise chosen must not tension the affected area.

Range-of-motion exercises
  1. Non-weight-bearing
     movements performed
     around affected area
	Must not tension the injured tissues. During the lag phase, these are used in elevation to decrease oedema.

Cardiovascular fitness	In the athlete it is important to maintain CV fitness; swimming can be used if pain free.
Maintenance programme	Because the horse will be resting, atrophy (muscle wastage) will occur in areas not directly associated with the primary site of tissue damage. Exercises should be given to prevent atrophy of these areas, and muscle stimulation to maintain nutrition and contractility is also used.

The use of electrotherapy during the lag phase:
Consider using electrotherapy once the haemorrhagic phase has ceased, that is, 24–48 hours post injury. The physiotherapist will use:

- ultrasound – usually pulsed;
- PWSD – pulsed short-wave therapy;
- laser (pictured below);
- interferential;
- TENS – transcutaneous electrical stimulation;
- RMC – rhythmical muscle contractions – muscle stimulation.

Using laser treatment on a shoulder injury

18

Phase 2: The Regeneration Phase

GLOSSARY OF TERMS

Fibroblasts: Densely and loosely arranged cells that produce collagen, which forms the basis of tendons, joint capsules, ligaments and scar tissue.

Proprioceptor: A specialised sensory nerve ending that monitors internal changes in the body brought about by movement and muscular activity.

WHAT HAPPENS?

The regeneration phase usually commences at approximately day five post injury, and it lasts for approximately three weeks, depending on the severity of the tissue trauma. It is during this phase that collagen synthesis occurs, and is therefore the time that tensile strength begins to increase.

TREATMENT

There are seven aims of treatment during this phase:

Primary site injury

1 To promote collagen orientation and synthesis at the site of tissue damage.

2 To restore range of motion to the affected area.

Non-injured areas

3 To restore muscular strength, power and endurance.

4 To restore self-awareness and confidence (proprioception).

5 To restore co-ordination.

6 To restore skill-related activity.

7 To restore cardiovascular fitness.

The techniques used in the treatment of 1 and 2 must be to the point of slight discomfort only.

The techniques used in the treatment of 3 to 7 must be pain free.

Aim 1: Collagen Orientation and Synthesis

The fibroblasts, which play a key role in the synthesis and 'laying down' of collagen fibres, are unaware of the tissue they are in, and as a result they lay down collagen haphazardly. This will ultimately lead to a weak scar, which will limit movement and lead to re-injury. However, if the healing tissue is subjected to *carefully* applied tension along the lines of normal stress, the synthesis and orientation of collagen will be most suited to give the best functional outcome. As collagen synthesis usually reaches its maximum at approximately day 14 post injury, prior to day 14 all movements that tension the wound *must be pain free*, to avoid re-injury. After day 14, all movements that cause tension can do so to the point of slight resistance, thus causing the horse some discomfort (though this would be minimal).

KEY POINTS:

- Because at the end of day 21 the wound will have received just about as much collagen as it is going to receive, this time period of 5–21 days after a mild to moderate injury is important. Treatment by careful wound tensioning will mean that there is more collagen in the wound by day 21, and that the collagen is orientating along the normal lines of stress. This means that the tensile strength of the wound will be greater than had treatment (tension) not been applied – and this promotes an earlier return to function.
- Laser, ultrasound and PEME (pulsed electro-magnetic energy) have all been shown to increase the rate of collagen synthesis during this time period, and are therefore a useful adjunct to treatment.

Without tension = random orientation of collagen = weakness

With tension = collagen orientated along straight lines = strength

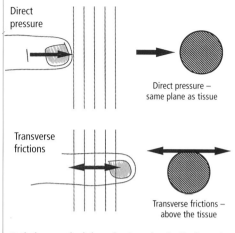

Direct pressure

Direct pressure –
same plane as tissue

Transverse frictions

Transverse frictions –
above the tissue

Both these methods bow the tissue longitudinally and therefore subject it to longitudinal tension which will help orientate the collagen fibres

3 Transverse frictions.
4 Combinations (of 1 and 2, and 1 and 3).
Transverse frictions are applied to restore soft tissue mobility, but unlike direct pressure, they are applied in a way that is superficial to the tissue. The difference between transverse frictions and direct pressure can be likened to the difference between pushing and rolling your finger over some cocktail sticks on a table (see diagram at left):
- frictions: finger rubbed back and forwards over the sticks;
- : direct pressure: pushing the cocktail sticks across the table.

Manual therapy ways of promoting collagen orientation:
Four methods exist:
1 Passive longitudinal stretching using physiological and accessory joint movements.
2 Direct pressure techniques.

KEY POINTS:
- Direct pressure techniques are more specific than transverse frictions.
- Great care has to be taken when applying tension to damaged tissue; too much tension will cause tissue disruption, and will restart the inflammatory reaction.

Above: Using transverse frictions on the brachiocephalic muscle

Below: Applying direct pressure to the gluteal muscle

GUIDELINES FOR THE APPLICATION OF SOFT TISSUE MOBILISATIONS

	Transverse frictions	Direct pressure	Long stretch
Time of application re- the healing process	Post day 14	Post day 5	Post day 5
Degree of pressure	Till day 21 pain free	Day 0–14 = pain free Day 14 + into resistance. Slight discomfort experienced by patient	As for direct pressure
Length of time pressure applied	Progress from small time of application eg 3 x 30 secs to minutes, past day 21	As for transverse frictions	As for transverse frictions

Aim 2: To Restore Range of Motion to the Affected Area

Following injury, the range of movement of that tissue and its associated structures is usually decreased.

Treatment following injury is to restore normal movement. Transverse frictions, direct pressure and longitudinal stretch restore motion to the primary site of tissue damage. As well as using manual therapy to restore motion, it is essential that the horse performs some active range-of-motion exercises to maintain and increase mobility between treatment sessions.

KEY POINTS:
- In some injuries the range of motion will be increased, for example, in the event of suspensory rupture. In these cases, any attempt to increase mobility would be detrimental to function.
- Do not mobilise joints that are in any way excessively mobile in function.
- Do not mobilise arthritic joints, either acute or chronic, without veterinary consultation.

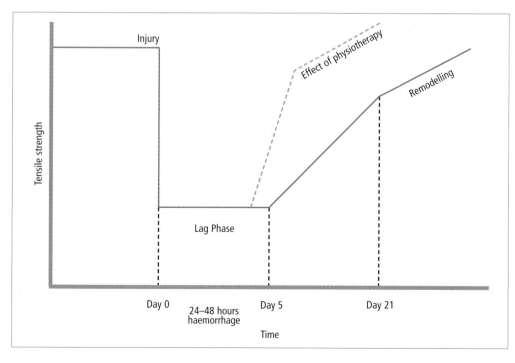

Aim 3: To Restore Muscular Strength, Power and Endurance

Following injury, some degree of muscular atrophy will almost inevitably occur, because the muscle is not being used, and because the horse feels inhibited due to the pain he feels. In your rehabilitation programme you need to restore strength, power and endurance, and it is important to do so without aggravating the primary site of tissue damage.

Muscular strength can be restored by removal of inflammatory exudate, using muscle stimulation and by keeping a careful check on nutrition

KEY POINTS:

- All regimes designed to develop muscular strength, power or endurance must be performed without causing pain. If pain occurs during the performance of the exercise, the horse will be too inhibited to continue making the effort, and so muscular development will not take place.

  Consider the following when designing a muscular development programme:
  - Progress from isometric (repeated, passive) to dynamic (active, self-induced) exercise.
  - Begin with endurance work (the number of repetitions should be greater than 12–15).
  - Progress to strength work (the number of repetitions should be less than 12).
  - Progress to power work (a time factor – limit — should be included).
- If the primary site of tissue damage is muscular, do not begin isometric contraction till after day five, and at all times the contractions used must not cause pain.
- Try to make the exercises as functional as possible for your horse's particular discipline; also try to use different movements with lots of changes to prevent fatigue.

Aim 4: Develop Self-Awareness and Self-Confidence (Proprioception)

Once the patient can bear weight through the limb, self-confidence can be developed. Gradually take the horse from a position of stability to one of instability by, for example, progressing from a stable base to an unstable one, using slopes, uneven surfaces, transferring weight.

> **KEY POINT:** Remember that two types of balance exist, static and dynamic. In the later stages of rehabilitation you should work on dynamic balance: you could use, for instance, cavaletti, raised poles. It is essential that these activities do not cause pain.

Pole work can be utilised for dynamic suppling and to improve co-ordination

Aim 5: Develop Co-ordination

This links in with the above 'proprioceptive' activities. Progress from simple to complex tasks. For example, first use poles on the floor, then progressively raise them up; use them in a star-shaped pattern, also at uneven heights, and over uneven and different surfaces. Try to make the co-ordination activity progressively more functional.

Aim 6: Develop Skill-Related Activities

It is important that the equine athlete returns progressively to his functional level of activity. During the time of injury he will lose some of the activity-related skills that he has developed. In particular, timing is often affected. It is important to analyse the movements that are required for that horse's particular discipline, and then to begin a progressive programme to restore him to the pre-activity level.

For example, a cross-country driving horse could be schooled through cones or poles as part of its rehabilitation programme.

> **KEY POINT:** Towards the later stages of the programme you will probably work closely with your trainer, who will be more knowledgeable regarding specialist technique requirements.

Opposite: Treadmills are useful for gait re-education and they also allow the horse to be exercised without the weight of the rider

Aim 7: Maintain and Develop Cardiovascular Fitness

For the athlete, injury results in a decrease in cardiovascular fitness. Every effort should be made to prevent this decrease by keeping the athlete as active as possible, but *without aggravating* the primary site of tissue damage. Consider activities such as:

- Water treadmill
- Swimming
- Horse walker

Swimming allows the horse to be exercised without having to bear weight on injured limbs

24

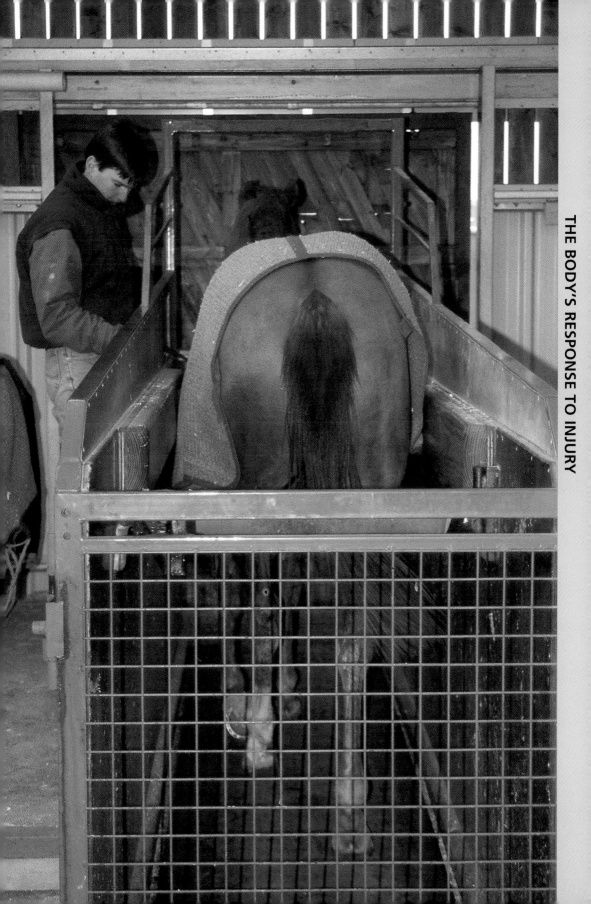

Phase 3: The Remodelling Phase

WHAT HAPPENS?

By the time the remodelling phase occurs, the scar tissue in the wound is well formed and will be starting to contract – and contracture of scar tissue will result in a decrease of tissue movement, which in turn will result in dysfunction. Furthermore, because scar tissue will continue to contract, it is essential that the horse, especially the athlete, continues to stretch the area on a regular basis, both dynamically and passively, if he is to restore his status quo.

TREATMENT

During this phase the direct pressure, longitudinal stretch and frictions techniques used will be performed to the point of minimal to moderate discomfort because the wound contains sufficient collagen to tension it. The aims of treatment during this phase are the same as those in the previous phase, but the therapies used make greater demands in order to counteract the more established healing process, so as to restore the horse's body structure to its full capability. To reiterate, the aims are these:

1 To promote collagen orientation and synthesis at the site of tissue damage.

2 To restore range of motion to the affected area.

3 To restore muscular strength, power and endurance.

4 To restore self-awareness and self-confidence (proprioception).

5 To restore co-ordination.

6 To restore skill-related activity.

7 To restore cardiovascular fitness.

CHRONIC INJURIES

Some horses will not have been diagnosed or have received treatment for some months post injury. This means that the healing process has already occurred, and in many cases because no treatment has been administered during the inflammatory or regeneration phase, the wound has healed, but with random collagen orientation, plus wound contracture and the formation of restrictive adhesions. Treatment in these cases will concentrate on those points where the soft tissue restriction lies, and aims to restore normal movement. Moreover, all the techniques used will cause mild to moderate discomfort, since enough tension has to be applied to influence the scar tissue.

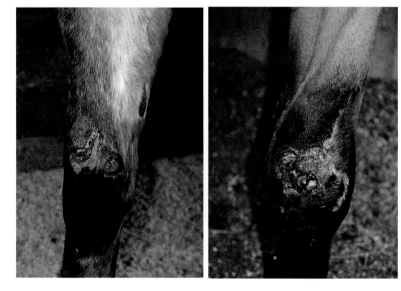

Some wounds can present problems with healing if not dealt with properly from the outset

Methods of
Diagnosis

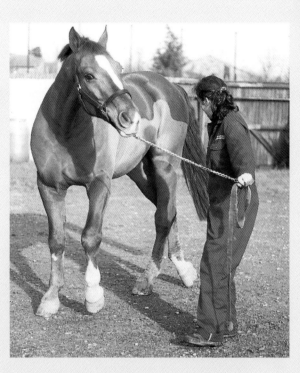

Before any form of treatment can be decided upon, the character and exact location of the horse's pain must be identified. The methods of diagnosis range from the 'hands-on' tests such as flexion tests or palpation, to the more scientific investigations involving blood tests and procedures such as radiography, ultrasonography and thermography. A high proportion of horse injury involves lameness, caused by damage to the structure of a limb. There are several ways by which a vet will try to isolate the seat of the trouble; these include flexion tests, nerve blocking and testing the reflexes.

Routine Tests to Isolate Pain

FLEXION TESTS

Flexion tests are carried out on the joint to test for pain. In this test the vet holds up each leg in turn so that it is flexed, and holds it in that position for a minute or so; the horse is then made to trot away immediately. Holding the leg in the flexed position causes compression of the structures, and if this causes pain or stiffness, the horse will move off with lame strides. Variable degrees of flexion can be applied. However, since isolation to one joint is hard to achieve, the test can provide erroneous information.

A flexion test of the forelimb. All the lower limb joints are being flexed but more stretch is being applied to the hoof

INTRA- AND EXTRA-ARTICULAR NERVE BLOCKS

Local anaesthetic is injected into the tissue or joint, to produce a numbing effect. After a small period of time, the horse is then trotted off, lunged or ridden to see if this has isolated the area of pain: the horse will move better, or differently, if the nerve block has numbed an area of pain.

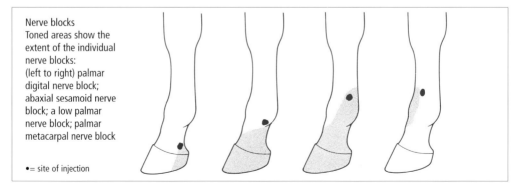

Nerve blocks
Toned areas show the extent of the individual nerve blocks:
(left to right) palmar digital nerve block; abaxial sesamoid nerve block; a low palmar nerve block; palmar metacarpal nerve block

•= site of injection

REFLEXES

Using a blunt object or the finger nails, the practitioner will palpate the horse in such a way as to produce a rapid movement response. This is testing normal response time and the ability to produce the movement. The local tissues are also observed for any indication of pain, such as muscle guarding.

> **KEY POINT:** If the horse is stiff and has reduced range of motion, these reflexes are used as an exercise to help develop the mobility of the spine.

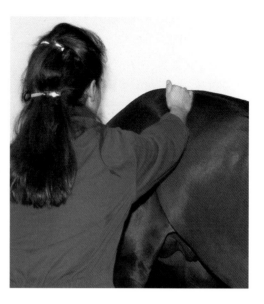

Right: Reflex testing. A normal response is being observed when the horse lifts its back and rounds the buttocks on the quarters reflex test

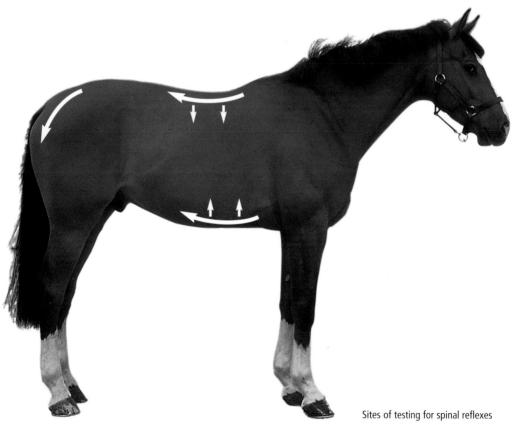

Sites of testing for spinal reflexes

PASSIVE MOVEMENTS

This part of the assessment is to establish the available range of motion, and to ascertain the freedom with which that movement range can be accomplished. Some movements have a different feel – for instance, a hard block as in joint damage — and this is detected by an experienced clinician. Care is needed in interpreting the resistance or refusal to allow a certain movement. The source of discomfort may lie in the limb you are moving, in the limb that has been forced to bear more weight, or because the horse is trying to adapt its position in response to the intervention. The horse may also be apprehensive of the handling of a limb that has been painful in the past.

Assessment of the horse's movement is part of the early work-up in treating lameness. Working the horse over different surfaces may change the way he moves

TESTING FOR LAMENESS

The tests outlined below are generally performed by the veterinary surgeon. When the horse is standing still he will evaluate it for the following things:

- Conformation, and in what ways the horse varies from normal, and the effects of these.
- Stance: whether the horse is standing with equal weight on its four limbs.
- Overall muscular development, with particular attention to signs of hypertrophy / atrophy.
- The condition of the skin, and whether it is dry, or dull, or shiny.
- The overall body condition.

He will then proceed to evaluate the horse's condition when it is in movement: on a hard, level surface he will assess it from halt to walk, in walk, from walk to trot, at trot, and from trot to walk. He will pay particular attention to how the transitions are performed; the transfer of bodyweight; the length of stride; the carriage of the limbs; and the overall aesthetic quality.

He will then assess it on a circle, on a hard surface: this can be in hand or on the lunge, when he will watch out for all the above points. The hard surface will help to identify a weight-bearing lameness, as it will be exacerbated by the concussive effects of the surface.

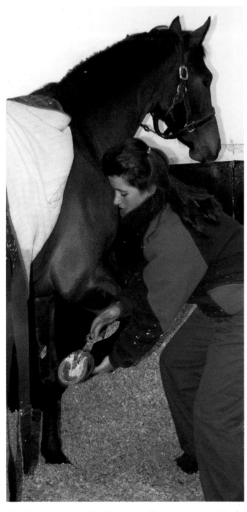

Passive movements. The joint and soft tissues are stretched to assess freedom and range of motion

He may then assess it in the same way on a circle, but on a soft surface; this may point up muscle and soft tissue injuries.

For the horse with suspected back pain the vet may ask for a roller to be put on, when he will carry out all the above tests on the lunge. He might also ask for the horse to be ridden; in particular he will watch for the horse's reaction when it is tacked up, and when the rider gets on, and how it behaves when it is asked to move off.

SPECIFIC TESTS

Certain tests will reveal pain and impaired mobility in particular areas of the body:

- Lungeing on an incline, both up- and downhill, will increase any lameness.
- Reining back on a hill, up- and downhill, will establish stifle, pelvic or low back pain.
- Performing 'figures-of-eight' in hand will reveal sacroiliac problems.
- Short turns, right and left, will show the extent of the body's mobility, and equally if there is any compromised ability.
- Short turns, described very fast, will test response and awareness of the body and limb placement, and will show up neurological problems.

- Picking up the opposite hind leg, and watching to see how the horse copes with balancing himself on three legs, tests for pelvic stability.

Observation of overall flexibility and the ability to cross and transfer weight on the hindlimbs is observed while turning the horse on a short circle

Pelvic stability test. The hosre is placed against a fence for safety and the opposite hindlimb is mobilised. If weakness is present the horse may not want the hindlimb to be elevated, or the weight-bearing limb may buckle or sway

TESTING FOR NEUROLOGICAL PROBLEMS

The tail-sway test: The way the horse carries its tail, and how the tail moves when the horse moves, is an indication of the horse's neurological status. Thus, when the horse is walked up and down, its tail should sway an equal amount on each side of its body.

When the tail is pulled to one side, the horse should counter-pull away.

The tail-sway test is used to detect neurological problems

The blindfold test: Again, this tests the horse's neurological status. The vet will ask for the horse to be turned short, and then to walk forwards, and he will watch to see if the horse's self-awareness and mobility are impaired with the blindfold in place.

PALPATION

Touch is used to ascertain the temperature, consistency and reactivity of the tissues. Deep palpation will be used to 'feel' larger muscles and more deeply located structures. A light to medium palpation touch has to be used to assess

superficial pain and tone. Some horses are naturally more sensitive or 'tickly' and may require a period of de-sensitising (by stroking the area first), before the practitioner is able to interpret their response.

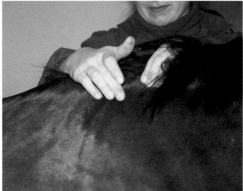

Palpation. This is done to detect tone, sensitivity, oedema and scar tissue

Diagnosis Through Scientific Methods

RADIOGRAPHY

X-rays are a means of making bone structures visible. They provide information about:

- the spacing between joints;
- the presence of fractures;
- the development of spurs of bone or arthritis (inflammation of the bone).

There has to be a bone mass reduction of at least 40 per cent before x-rays will show visible damage, before the changes are apparent on x-ray. This can take up to six weeks from the onset of injury. This can mean that an x-ray taken in isolation may not lead to a clear diagnosis. They are only two dimensional, whereas the horse's body is three dimensional, and dynamically changing.

X-ray quality can also be variable, and although portable equipment is used if it is safe and practical to do so, on-site facilities at an equine hospital may be more revealing. X-rays should form part of a comprehensive evaluation, comparing their information with other diagnostic tools and a clinical examination. It is important to establish the exact location of the pain, and then carry out the diagnostic testing.

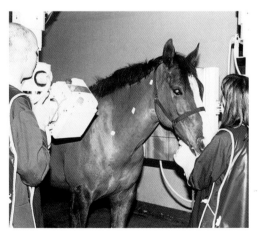

Radiography combined with a clinical examination will give valuable information on the state of the skeleton

ULTRASONOGRAPHY

Ultrasound scanning has a wide application, from pregnancy diagnosis to detecting lesions in tendons and ligaments. It works by measuring the echo of ultrasound waves, which bounce off surfaces around them. Diagnostic ultrasound waves are absorbed and reflected differently by the various kinds of tissue. Separation of fibres and areas of haemorrhage can be deduced from any lack of uniformity in the reflected ultrasound beam. They are therefore used to monitor healing and should be repeated during the healing process.

It is a painless procedure, in which a couplant is applied to the area to be scanned; the hair may be clipped to allow a clearer picture.

THERMOGRAPHY

This is becoming more widely used, but there are still some concerns over its correct application, and the interpretation and significance of the thermographic images.

Carried out in environmentally controlled conditions by an experienced clinician, information may be obtained about the surface skin temperature of the horse at the time it is imaged. Thermographic patterns are being used to study the effects of trauma on the musculoskeletal system.

Neuromuscular disease is believed by its proponents to be a common, but often undiagnosed, cause of chronic pain and performance problems in horses. Thermographic imaging reveals patterns of long-standing irritation in the back and neck caused by pressure on the nerve root. This leads to 'cold spots', and is often seen some time after the original trauma. 'Hot spots' reveal acute inflammation, as in recent problems.

Thermography in practice is interpreted alongside other diagnostic imaging, and also with the clinical examination. The technique is non-invasive and requires the horse to be clean, dry and unstressed. Before being imaged, the horse should be standing in an examination room whose

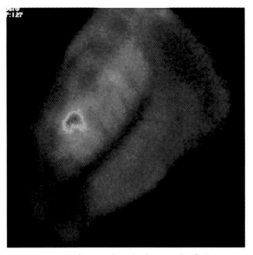

Gamma scintigraphy reveals active bone and soft tissue inflammation

MAGNETIC RESONANCE IMAGING (MRI)

MRI produces exquisite images of tissues, which could not previously be imaged, and yields image slices through any plane desired. It can therefore characterise subtle pathological changes in a variety of tissues. It is still very specialised and only available at certain equine referral hospitals, so it may not be part of the norm for all veterinary lameness evaluation at present.

ARTHROSCOPY

This is a surgical procedure that is performed under general anaesthetic, and is used to explore the joint and visualise the contents. It is invasive, and it is limiting in some of its information. In the past it was considered the 'gold standard' for joint evaluation.

ambient temperature is carefully controlled. The camera is held at a distance from the horse, and the images are recorded on a screen.

GAMMA SCINTIGRAPHY

This is an invaluable tool for identifying early bone lesions and soft tissue injuries (if used in the soft tissue phase). The horse has to be admitted to hospital, normally for several days. A radioactive marker substance is injected into the bloodstream, and the way the bones and soft tissues take it up is monitored.

Bone can be remodelled after fractures; in response to inflammation; and in response to mechanical overload. The marker substance accumulates wherever this remodelling is taking place, and by using a bone scan these hot spots can be located. Once the scan has identified an area as a potential problem, the use of x-rays for bone and ultrasound for ligaments will be required to further diagnose the problems.

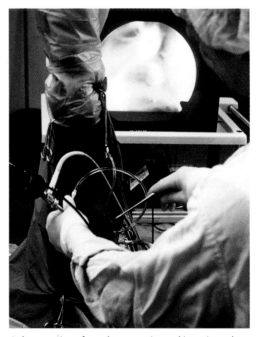

Arthroscopy is performed to assess internal integrity and to flush out debris and remove damaged bone

The Causes of Injury and its Treatment

In this chapter we first consider the relationship between a horse's conformation and its potential for athletic performance, and equally, to what extent its conformation predisposes it to injury. We then consider the conditions and injuries that very often beset the active working horse, and how to recognise the symptoms for each one, and thereby isolate the seat of pain; and finally we explore the best ways to treat and manage that condition.

Conformation

GLOSSARY OF TERMS
Phalanges: Made up of the first, second and third phalanges – the pastern, coronary and pedal bones.
Medial: Inside the limb edge.
Distal: Anatomical reference meaning farther from a given point ie a bone farthest away from the body, or vessel farthest from the heart.

Conformation describes the main shape and make-up of the horse, and the skeleton is the main structure that determines conformation. Differences in conformation are therefore determined by an infinite variation in the size and shape of the bones, and the angles they make with one another. Traditionally, assessments of conformation highlight individual anatomical structures, but an overall appraisal of the horse should be the first consideration.

• **Conformation** determines **type:**

• **Type** influences the most suitable **use**:
• **Use** influences the farriery requirement.

• **Conformation** influences **athletic potential,**
  which influences the **ability to withstand physical stress,**
  which determines the **position of the centre of gravity,**
  which influences the **horse's action,**
  which influences its **suitability for breeding purposes.**

Hoof/pastern axis (HPA): There should be a straight line through the phalanges when viewed from the side (laterally). The HPA should relate closely to the angle of the shoulder, and it will affect both stride length and elevation of the limb. Hind-leg HPA should also be straight, normally slightly steeper (approximately 5 per cent) than the forelimb.

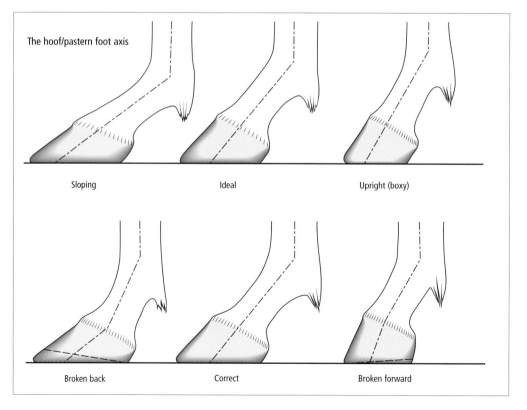

The hoof/pastern foot axis

Sloping   Ideal   Upright (boxy)

Broken back   Correct   Broken forward

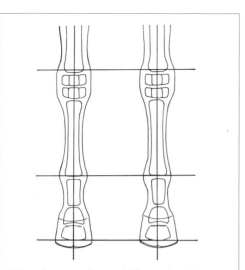

Bi-lateral symmetry is essential for equal weight distribution

Bi-lateral symmetry: This is possibly the most important point of conformation. It helps to ensure that load and wear are equal on each paired structure, and is particularly important when considering the limbs and feet. Symmetry helps to ensure that the flight path of the foot is parallel to the longitudinal axis of the horse.

Position of the hock: A vertical line downwards from the point of the quarter should pass slightly behind and parallel to the flexor tendons from the point of the hock to the fetlock.

Weight distribution: Weight should be loaded as approximately 60 per cent forelimb and 40 per cent hind limb.

Good conformation is important as weaknesses can predispose the horse to injury and disease. Short-backed horses (left) are more prone to spinal disease, eg dorsal spine impingement while long-backed horses (below) suffer more soft tissue injuries

CONFORMATION AND LAMENESS

The following table comprises a list of some of the more common conformation abnormalities encountered, and the detrimental effect that they have on the horse's soundness.

Conformation problems can play a major part in the origins of lameness and spinal problems in the horse. To get a full picture of the possible limb origins of some of the spinal problems you might encounter, it is important to study the animal carefully when it is standing – from the front, back, and each side – and when it is walked and trotted up.

GAIT IRREGULARITIES

Lameness may be caused by certain nervous disorders, and the two most commonly seen are stringhalt and shivering.

STRINGHALT

The horse hyperflexes one or both hocks. It normally affects adult horses. The onset of the affliction is gradual, but the condition generally becomes progressively worse.

Cause

Traditional stringhalt is not well understood, but a type of stringhalt in Australia is caused by a plant toxin.

ABNORMALITIES	CONSEQUENCE
Base wide, toe out	Medial wear and winging
Base wide, toe in	Medial wear and paddle
Base narrow, toe out	Lateral wear and winging and plaiting
Base narrow, toe in	Lateral wear and paddle

Poor pastern conformation:
    Short upright
    Long upright
	
	Fetlock injuries, ringbone and navicular disease
	Fetlock injuries and navicular disease

Poor pastern angulation	Ideally 45° front and 50° behind
	    Too much angulation predisposes to bowed tendons
	    Too little results in poor shock absorption
	    Medial aspect approx 3in below carpus – due to hard training,
	        poor conformation

Sickle hocks	Lateral view, curvature is too great
Post-legged	Lateral view, legs too straight
Capped hock	Traumatic in origin
Thoroughpin	Seen in active young horses – excess bursal effusions
Bog spavin	On the medial aspect of the hock – denotes injury or stress to the joint
Bone spavin	Osteoarthritis of hock joint
Cow-hocked	Hocks too close when viewed from behind – stresses the medial aspects of the limb
Bandy-hocked	Hocks too far apart – stresses the lateral aspects of the limb

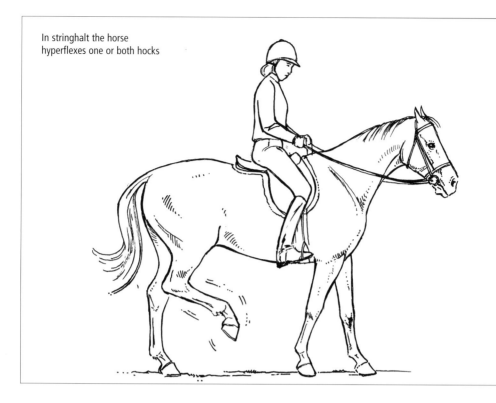

In stringhalt the horse hyperflexes one or both hocks

Signs

There is exaggerated flexion of one or both hind legs, and in the Australian version, also the forelegs. It is most apparent at walk, but can be intermittent and may disappear at trot. The condition can remain static, or it can deteriorate.

Treatment:

Some horses have surgery to the lateral digital extensor tendon at the level of the hock.

> **KEY POINT:** Most horses are able to continue to work, though with a varying degree of mechanical lameness; dressage is the only discipline where such altered movement is not acceptable. Surgery can help, but it is not guaranteed.

SHIVERING

The hindleg is picked up and held, and shakes. This reaction can be produced by making the horse go backwards, or by asking him to pick up his leg. It is seen in the larger breeds, but is rare. Most can still perform, but the condition may become worse, and it can always cause functional difficulties, such as when being shod, or when putting on studs at a competition.

THE CONFORMATION OF THE FOOT

Assessing the Horse's Foot

- Make sure he is on a level surface and standing square.
- A radiograph is required to appreciate the pedal bone's position and to make a perpendicular line dropped from the centre of rotation of the coffin joint.
- Palpation of the centre of rotation of the fetlock joint is an important anatomical point.

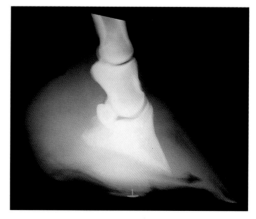

Radiographs are required to assess internal symmetry

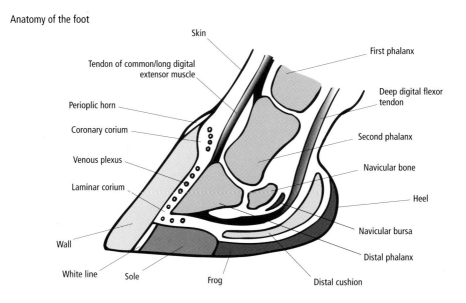

Anatomy of the foot

Skin

First phalanx

Tendon of common/long digital extensor muscle

Deep digital flexor tendon

Perioplic horn

Coronary corium

Second phalanx

Venous plexus

Navicular bone

Laminar corium

Heel

Wall

Navicular bursa

Distal phalanx

White line   Sole   Frog

Distal cushion

Distal phalanx

- The deep digital flexor tendon passes over the back of the navicular bone and inserts into the distal phalanx.

- Attached to the sides of the distal phalanx are the cartilages of the foot. These can become ossified (side bone).

- The distal phalanx is supported in the foot by laminae. Sensitive laminae are attached to the distal phalanx and interdigitate with the insensitive laminae (that line the inside of the hoof wall).

- The white line is seen on the sole of the foot and represents the division between the sensitive and insensitive laminae.

- The wall of the foot is horny tissue secreted by the coronary band; it is produced at a rate of 1cm per month. The walls are covered by a thin membrane that controls the movement of moisture into and out of the wall.

- The frog acts as a cushion to prevent the total drop of the sole, and restricts the spread of the heels.

FOOT CONDITIONS

Condition	Cause	Signs	Treatment
Bruised feet	Thin-soled Flat-footed	Lame on hard ground	Cold hosing NSAID
Corn	Bruise which occurs between the wall and bar of the foot at the seat of corn	Lame	Cold hosing Laser Corrective shoeing
Foot imbalance	Too long between shoeings. Poorly balanced feet initially. **Key point:** *Studs can cause imbalance if worn on hard ground and if only on one side*	Can become lame due to unequal load-bearing through foot	Correct foot imbalance Ensure horse is shod (regularly)

Pony showing typical laminitic stance

The axis of the foot is determined by an 'imaginary' or 'actual' straight line taken through the phalanges and hoof from the approximate centre of the fetlock joint. This line should then be parallel with the angle of the wall at the toe and the slope of the buttress at the heels.

Foot Pain

Whatever its cause, pain in the feet will result in an abnormal gait and will eventually lead to lameness. It will affect the horse's whole way of going, and will severely compromise his muscle tone and fitness, and his ability to work.

Wedges and Pads

Wedges are used by some to correct the hoof/pastern axis. However, any good farrier will tell you that applying heel wedges is unnecessary and often inadvisable because they provide only a short-term solution in cases where the heels have collapsed. Furthermore the continued use of wedges will ultimately crush the horn tubules at the heel even more.

Pads should only be worn if the horse has suffered a punctured sole prior to competition. They do little to alter the concussing force transmitted through the foot. Moreover they can cause problems because correct fitting becomes difficult, and also bacterial infections may develop underneath the pads.

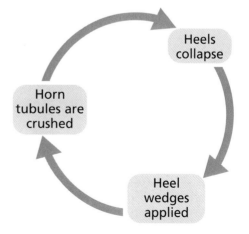

Vicious spiral of heel collapse as the result of wedges being applied

DIFFERENT EQUINE DISCIPLINES AND HOW THEY PREDISPOSE TO INJURY

Discipline	Injury	Cause
Flat racing	Condylar fractures of metacarpal head	Working on all-weather surfaces
	Erosions of head of first phalanx	Working on hard ground
	Microfractures	Repeated stress on immature limbs
	Chronic stress fractures	Continuous training without resting original injury
	Myofascial pain	Secondary to pathology of limbs
	Pelvic strains	Jumping off fast
Endurance	Sclerosis of the third carpal bone	Repetitive trauma
	Muscle soreness	Fatigue
National Hunt horses	Tendons (SDFT)	Fatigue and overuse
	Upper part of suspensory ligament	Jumping
	Sacroiliac strain	Jumping
Eventers	Low branches suspensory ligament	Overuse
	Whiplash	Falls onto head
	Torsional strains	Can occur over drop fences
Showjumpers	SDFT	Overloading
	DDFT	Overloading
	Chronic strain of distal check ligament	Overuse
	Iliopsoas muscle strains	Slipping on tight turns
	Gluteal muscle strains	Effort of height of fences and speed classes
Dressage	Suspensory ligaments, especially hindlimbs	Strain of the movements
	Thoracolumbar stiffness	Nature of athletic activity

GLOSSARY OF TERMS

Condyle: Rounded projection of bone **SDFT:** Superficial digital flexor tendon
DDFT: Deep digital flexor tendon **Thoracolumbar:** Spinal area behind saddle

Identifying and Treating Common Injuries

In the following section we investigate the injuries that are most commonly incurred by the horse, also how to recognise the symptoms for each condition, and finally we consider the best ways to treat and manage that condition.

CONDITIONS OF BONE

SPLINT

A splint is a bony enlargement of one of the small metacarpal or metatarsal bones. It is the result of a slight tearing of the interosseous ligament between the splint bone and the cannon bone, and this injury also lifts the periosteum to which the ligament is attached. The movement between the splint and cannon bones, and the resulting inflammation of the interosseous ligament and periosteum, causes pain and soft tissue swelling. Some calcification of the ligament occurs, and new bone is produced beneath the elevated periosteum. In the end, a firmer union between the splint and cannon bone develops. It can occur in both the front and the hind limbs, although the former is more common.

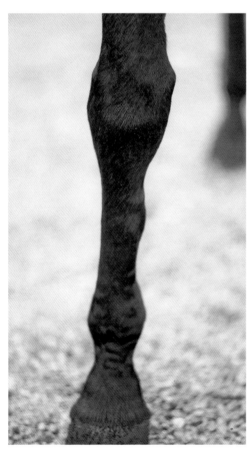

A splint on the medial aspect of the metacarpal bone

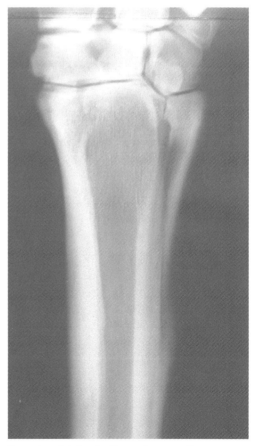

X-ray of a splint showing the new bone growth on the right

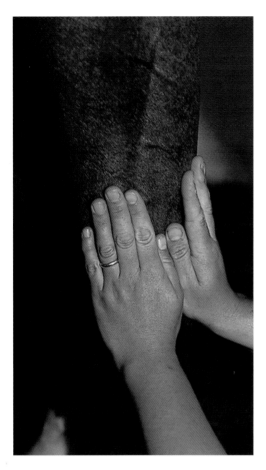
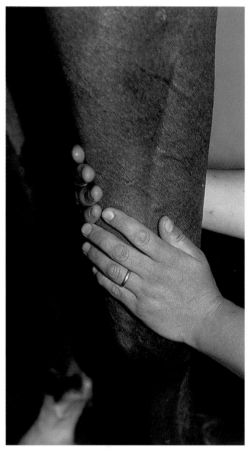

Causes
- Poor conformation, for example bench knees, or moving too closely, when it is self-inflicted.
- Improper trimming of the foot, causing uneven foot placement.
- Incorrect phosphorous:calcium ratio in the diet.
- Trauma, for example a kick.
- Working on excessively hard ground.

Signs/Symptoms
The horse is lame: this can vary from mild to moderate lameness at trot, and it is worse on hard ground. There is palpable swelling early on caused by acute inflammation, however this becomes progressively harder due to a bony and fibrous reaction.

Diagnosis
Radiography can be useful, to determine if the

Massage to increase circulation can be effective in the treatment of splints

splint is active. The bony changes take 10–14 days to occur. It is important at this stage to eliminate a splint bone fracture.

Treatment
The aims of treatment are to help minimise the pain, and to enhance the resolution of the oedema (swelling). It is often advisable to restrict free exercise, especially if the ground is hard. Successful resolution also depends on identifying the cause – for instance, if the foot is unbalanced and is therefore causing stress on the bone.

In the acute stages, ice and laser therapies may be used, also massage.

In the chronic stages the effort should be to minimise the fibrous reaction.

Joints and their Structure

Articular cartilage covers the ends of the bones: it both protects, and transmits forces to, underlying bone. It has no nerve supply, so damage to it does not cause pain. Nor does it have a blood supply: it extracts nutrition from the synovial joint fluid.

It is vulnerable to damage if the synovial fluid is impaired for any reason, resulting in weakness and therefore decreased resistance to stress. It has limited powers of regeneration, and incompletely repairs.

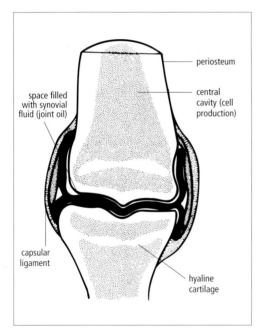

The synovial membrane controls the composition of synovial fluid. This consists of hyaluronic acid and some of the constituents of blood. The synovial membrane has a nerve and blood supply, and pain is caused by inflammation of this and the surrounding joint capsule. It is this that causes lameness. Synovial fluid is vital for the nutrition of the articular cartilage, and it is a lubricant of the synovial membrane and joint capsule.

There are various conditions of joints, some more readily treatable than others.

OSTEOCHONDROSIS
This condition is a developmental abnormality of the cartilage and bone that occurs in young, rapidly growing individuals. Most joints can be affected, and the signs usually occur within the first two years of life.

Signs/Symptoms
The affected joints swell, and the horse is lame; this is caused by the detaching cartilage, which stimulates inflammation within the joint and produces excess synovial fluid.

Diagnosis
Radiography (see p33) and arthroscopy (see p34) are used to confirm the disease.

Treatment
It is necessary to control the predisposing factors – for example, the nutritional intake – and to limit exercise. Surgery will be required to resolve the detached cartilage if lameness persists.

JOINT CAPSULE DISTENSIONS
ARTICULAR WINDGALLS
The joint will be enlarged, the thickening of the joint capsule or its distension caused by excessive synovial fluid. Often the horse is not lame.

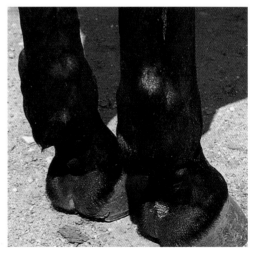

Windgalls

Causes

The breed type – middle- to heavyweight – will predispose to this condition, as will an upright forelimb.

Excessive work on hard ground is a causative factor.

Treatment

The first priority in any treatment programme is to remove the cause.

It is also important to treat the effects of hard work – for example, by cold hosing.

BOG SPAVIN

This is a distension of the joint capsule of the hock (tarsocrural/tibiotarsal); it does not always cause lameness. It is common in young, fast-growing youngsters.

Normally it resolves spontaneously, unless the distension reflects disease within the hock, such as OCD or a bone spavin.

If the horse is lame, radiography is required to help in diagnosis.

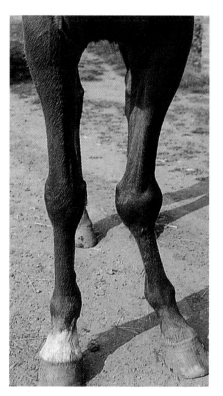

This horse's conformation has predisposed it to arthritic changes affecting the knee

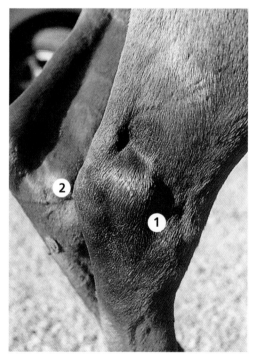

Bog spavin: swelling is most obviously apparent at the front and inside of the hock (1) but also at the outside of the hock (2). If pressure is applied to one swelling (1) the other (2) will enlarge

SECONDARY (DEGENERATIVE) JOINT DISEASE (DJD) (OSTEOARTHRITIS)

DJD is primarily a disease of cartilage, and may develop as a result of direct trauma, or as a consequence of faulty conformation, where abnormal stresses are placed on the joint. It affects both young and old horses.

Signs/Symptoms

Lameness can occur suddenly, or more slowly over a period of time. There may be swelling of the joints, and flexing a joint may be uncomfortable and increase the lameness. Eventually the joint becomes restricted because of thickening and scarring of the connective tissue due to the inflammation (fibrosis). There will be a firm swelling around the joint if new bone develops.

Diagnosis

Nerve blocks and radiographs may be indicated to identify the source of pain. However, it is worth noting that there is often a poor correlation between clinical signs and radiographic abnormalities. Besides, in the early stages no radiographic changes are detectable, so the use of local anaesthesia to determine pain will be more informative.

Treatment

The aims of treatment are to:

• minimise soft tissue inflammation and pain;
• improve joint lubrication;
• maintain optimal nutrition of articular cartilage.

In the acute stage of the condition this is done by.

• cold therapy
• massage
• passive movement
• veterinary medication
• reduced exercise

In certain circumstances the outcome is less hopeful:

• if there are conformational abnormalities;
• if the horse has been lame for some time;
• if there has been a considerable amount of bony change;
• if there is articular cartilage damage in the joint.

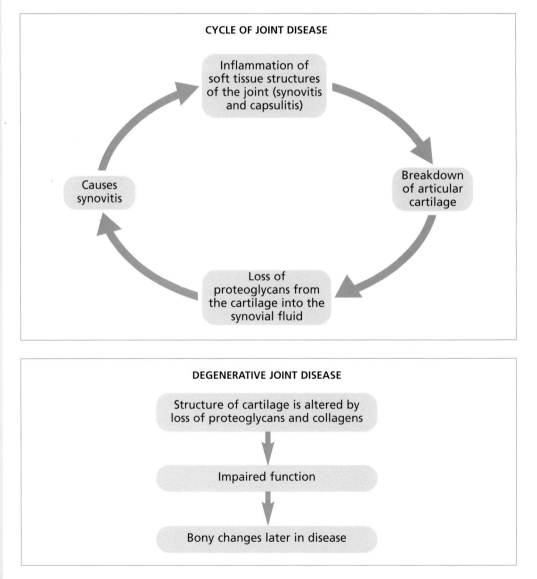

CYCLE OF JOINT DISEASE

Inflammation of soft tissue structures of the joint (synovitis and capsulitis)

Breakdown of articular cartilage

Loss of proteoglycans from the cartilage into the synovial fluid

Causes synovitis

DEGENERATIVE JOINT DISEASE

Structure of cartilage is altered by loss of proteoglycans and collagens

Impaired function

Bony changes later in disease

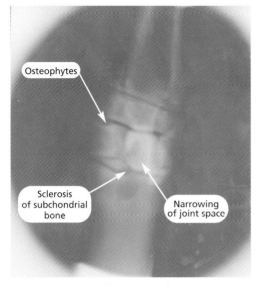

Radiographic changes of degenerative disease

KEY POINTS:
- The joint should not be completely immobilised, as this counteracts normal cartilage nutrition.
- The condition is incurable, so the earlier it is diagnosed the better, to prevent excessive continuing damage from a full work regime.

Medication may include the following:
- analgesic medication;
- complementary medication – eg acupuncture or homoeopathy;
- lubricants.

Note that analgesic medication helps to control the pain but is not a cure, so continually stressing an already damaged joint may accelerate its deterioration.

SECONDARY JOINT DISEASE OF HOCK:
BONE SPAVIN
The hock consists of lots of joints. The tarsocrural joint is the largest, and most flexion occurs here.

There is very little movement in the proximal distal intertarsal and the tarsocrural joints.

Bone spavin is the same as degenerative joint disease or osteoarthritis of the hock and is one of the most common causes of hind-limb lameness in the horse.

The bones in the hock that are most commonly affected are:

the distal intertarsal joint;
the tarsometatarsal joints.

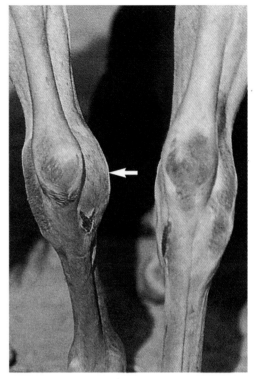

Firm swelling at the level of the distal intertarsal joint and tarsometatarsal joint. Fibrous reaction around the joints

The condition only occasionally involves the proximal intertarsal joint.

Signs/Symptoms
- Bone spavin often affects both limbs.
- Generalised stiffness that improves with exercise.
- Lack of hind-limb propulsion.
- Decreased flexibility on circles.
- Unlevel steps taken.
- Loss of rhythm or lame strides in medium or extended paces.
- Refusing when jumping.
- An abnormal posture – restricted.

More general symptoms include:
- asymmetry of muscle development in the hindquarters;
- affected side less developed;
- altered gait, excessive toe wear, due to decreased flexion of the limb;
- the farrier may also notice restricted flexibility of the hind limbs;

49

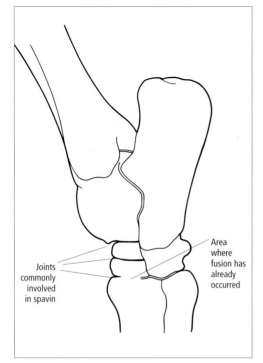

Joints commonly involved in spavin

Area where fusion has already occurred

Hock bones showing bone spavin

- palpable swelling on the inside of the hock may develop;
- the back muscles may become hypersensitive and tight as a result of trying to compensate for the affected limb.

Diagnosis

There are three main ways in which this condition may be identified: radiographic examination, veterinary examination, and nerve blocks.

Radiographic examination: Nature appears to try to stabilize the joints by producing new bone to bridge the joints. This in theory removes the source of pain.

Veterinary examination: The flexion test may exacerbate the lameness, but not always. A gait analysis and clinical examination are the most helpful.

Nerve blocks: These confirm the area of pain, but the lameness must be obvious enough to show significant change after the nerve blocks.

Treatment

If the horse is rested, he will improve, but on return to work he will often go lame again. Treatment aims to accelerate the degenerative changes in order to help the stabilisation by fusion of the affected joints. Once fused, because the changes occur in the low motion joints, function – particularly flexion – will not be affected. If the horse is not too lame, it is often worked on phenylbutazone, providing pain relief. Some corrective shoeing can help, changing the horse's gait. Modification of the type of work is required, such as avoiding steep hills and deep going.

Medication of the affected joints can help, but it will only be temporary, and will need periodic 'topping up'.

Surgery may be the chosen option in very lame cases. The aim is to destroy some of the articular cartilage and to accelerate fusion of the joint.

A newer surgical procedure is to try and relieve pressure by drilling holes into the bones.

Tendons

Every time a horse lands after a jump he fully loads a forelimb into maximum extension. Here this is demonstrated on the near fore

STRUCTURE OF THE TENDON

The tendons of the lower limbs are long and have the ability to stretch and store energy, which is released when the foot is lifted from the ground. However, there are certain circumstances when the tendons will be susceptible to injury:

- when the horse is fatigued;
- when the ground is unstable, hard or holding;
- if the rider is too heavy;
- when jumping;
- when travelling at speed.

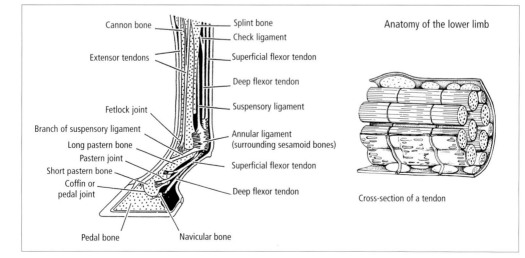

Cannon bone
Extensor tendons
Fetlock joint
Branch of suspensory ligament
Long pastern bone
Pastern joint
Short pastern bone
Coffin or pedal joint
Pedal bone

Splint bone
Check ligament
Superficial flexor tendon
Deep flexor tendon
Suspensory ligament
Annular ligament (surrounding sesamoid bones)
Superficial flexor tendon
Deep flexor tendon
Navicular bone

Anatomy of the lower limb

Cross-section of a tendon

51

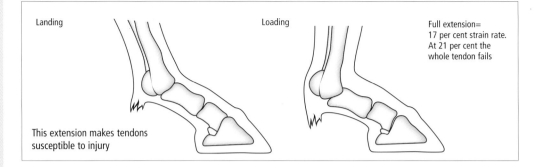

Landing

This extension makes tendons susceptible to injury

Loading

Full extension=
17 per cent strain rate.
At 21 per cent the
whole tendon fails

The tendon has a relatively good blood supply, and often when examined on injury is full of blood. The fibres exhibit 'crimp', meaning that rather than being straight, they bend in a regular zig-zag pattern; this gives the tendon a degree of elasticity. Normal tendon is composed of type 1 collagen, which is strong and elastic due to the complex arrangement of fibres within it. If damaged, repair tissue is formed from type 3 collagen, and is susceptible to re-injury.

It is an interesting fact that when older horses are (diagnostic) ultrasound scanned, most of them show evidence of some tendon damage in their forelimbs.

EXTERNAL INJURIES TO THE TENDONS

Topical injury may be caused by a direct blow, or the constriction caused by over-tight bandages; the latter may result in the 'bowing' of the superficial digital flexor tendon. The damage is not usually serious because the internal structure is not affected.

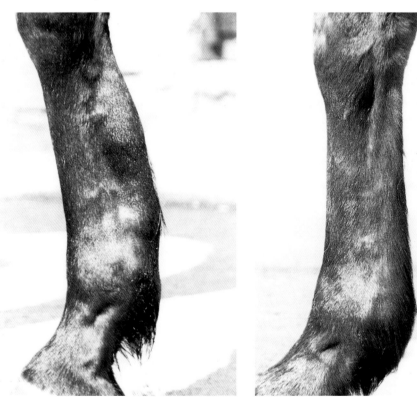

Tendon strain before treatment (left) and after (right)

Direct Blow
When a blow is suffered, rupture normally occurs in some of the internal structure. It repairs, but the quality of the scar tissue is inferior to the original.

TENDON STRAIN
When a tendon is strained, the normal pattern of fibrils and fibres is disrupted, with some rupture; the more severe the injury, the more fibres are damaged. Bleeding and inflammatory exudates cause more damage to the internal structure.

Causes
- Bad conformation
- High speed
- Fatigue
- Poor co-ordination
- Uneven terrain

Signs/Symptoms
Generally the horse is lame to some degree. However, significant tendon damage can occur without the horse being lame, but swelling of the leg should be an early warning sign.

Diagnosis
The vet will use an ultrasound scanner to diagnose the condition and investigate its severity, and in the course of treatment to provide regular monitoring of the healing process.

Treatment and Care
In acute cases, treatment will involve reducing the swelling by means of, for example, **cold therapy**, in order to minimise the inflammatory reaction. The more quickly the soft tissue swelling is resolved, the better the long-term prospects will be.

Physiotherapy may also play an important part in treatment; this may include:

- muscle stimulation;
- suppling exercises;
- therapeutic ultrasound to damaged area in all three stages of healing;
- massage.

In the long term, complete repair takes time. **Rest, combined with controlled exercise**, is essential. Note, too, that horses are often sound *before*

complete healing has been achieved, so early resumption of full work must be delayed.

DAILY ROUTINE
- Check the limb by observation and palpation.
- Compare each leg.
- Compare when weight-bearing, and when not weight-bearing.
- Squeeze each tendon gently between finger and thumb, starting at the top and working slowly downwards.
- Assess the consistency of the tendon.
- Assess the reaction of the horse to gentle pressure.

Prevention
- Regularly run a hand down the limbs.
- Avoid the causative factors, where possible (see Causes, at left).
- Avoid using exercise bandages: during high intensity exercise the temperature of the tissue often rises to extremely high levels, perhaps 40–45 degrees. If the legs are bandaged there exists a potential for further over-heating.
- Avoid fatigue, and exercising on uneven, deep going at speed.
- Cold hose the horse's legs to facilitate cooling after exercise; this practice may well help to minimise the risk of strain.

KEY POINT:
Cold hosing appears to be a physically more superior method of cooling, allowing effective heat exchange and reduction in core temperature.

Ligaments

Ligaments are fibrous bands that attach to bone. They are susceptible to injury such as a sprain.

THE SUSPENSORY LIGAMENT

This ligament is important in its role as part of the suspensory apparatus supporting the fetlock joint. It may be injured anywhere along its length. The top of the ligament cannot be directly felt, but if it is damaged there may be heat, and the medial palmar vein that runs down the inside of the limb may be enlarged. It is more commonly injured in the lower two-thirds of its length, and often at the point where it divides into two branches in the lower part of the limb.

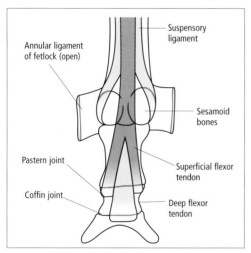

The suspensory apparatus supports the fetlock

- Annular ligament of fetlock (open)
- Suspensory ligament
- Sesamoid bones
- Pastern joint
- Superficial flexor tendon
- Coffin joint
- Deep flexor tendon

Signs/Symptoms

- If the ligament is recently damaged the leg will be thicker and soft to the touch.
- If the area is palpated with the leg off the ground it will be painful.
- The horse will be lame, though this may be very minor, and not apparent except after fast or excessive exercise. It will be lamer on a circle with the affected leg on the outside.

Diagnosis

- Local anaesthetic may help to localise the area.
- Radiographic examination may show signs of

damage at the site of the attachment of the suspensory ligament.
- An ultrasound scan will show the extent of damage.

Predisposing Causes

- Poor foot balance can be an aggravating factor. Maintaining a well balanced hoof is essential.
- Bad conformation: toe in or toe out conformation increases the risk of strain.
- Fast work: speed increases the risk.

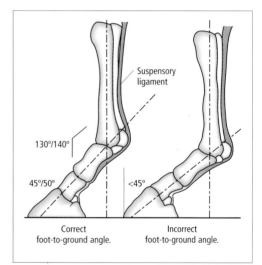

- Suspensory ligament
- 130°/140°
- 45°/50°
- <45°

Correct foot-to-ground angle. Incorrect foot-to-ground angle.

An incorrect foot-to-ground angle may predispose a horse to injury

Treatment

In the acute stages:
- Cold therapy
- Ultrasound
- Laser

In the chronic stages:
- Soft tissue mobilisation
- Electrotherapy
- Correction of predisposing factors

The horse's return to function depends on the predisposing factors, such as poor conformation and the required use of the horse.

Muscle Problems

Muscles control the movement of the body. They attach to the bone via tendons, and have a nerve supply and blood supply. Both are important for normal function.

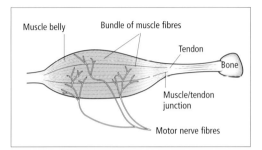

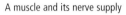

A muscle and its nerve supply

The three different forms of muscle action are:
1 concentric – shortening;
2 eccentric – lengthening;
3 isometric – static.

The most usual problems that beset muscles are caused by strain and/or fatigue.

MUSCLE STRAIN
Cause
• Overstretching of a fatigued muscle.
• Sudden incoordinate muscle contraction.

Signs/Symptoms
• Lameness: this is extremely variable, and depends on how much damage has been done, and which muscles are affected.
• Pain on palpation or on stretching the affected tissue.
• Swelling from inflammation can sometimes be palpated or seen.
• In chronic conditions evidence of injury can be provided from the texture of the tissue, and in some instances by a hole in the muscle itself.

As the injury becomes sub-acute to chronic, there will be muscle atrophy (wastage) and imbalance between the affected and the non-affected muscle groups.

This jumping sequence shows different types of muscle action: concentric (top photograph), eccentric (second) and isometric (third and fourth)

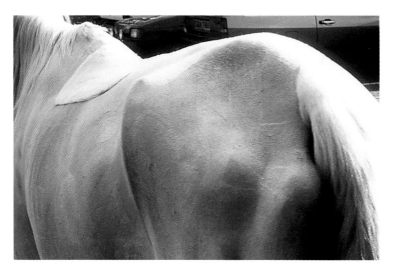

Atrophy of the hindquarters with the dip over the pelvis clearly visible

The areas most commonly affected are the pectorals, the hamstrings and the glutei.

Diagnosis

Palpation and passive movements of the muscle will help to identify pain and protective guarding. The use of muscle stimulation to identify pain and decreased muscle activity can be extremely helpful in confirming damage.

MUSCLE INJURIES AND DISEASES

The musculature of the horse is extensive, and its function is vital for everyday movement and ultimately athletic endeavour. Thus the assessment of muscular function is important, especially when stiffness or lameness is noted.

Fatigue

Fatigue indicates the inability of the animal to maintain a given level or intensity of activity. It is usually temporary, but sometimes can be prolonged. Signs of fatigue include the following:

- Rise in temperature
- Dehydration
- Depression
- Muscle cramps
- Shallow respiration
- Elevated heart rate
- Sweating.

Prolonged sweating (to dissipate the body heat) causes a potassium ion deficit. If the horse also has a glycogen depletion, as well as fatigue, death can result. Severe dehydration can lead to potassium deficit.

Treatment

The treatment for exhaustion is fluid and electrolyte therapy.

MUSCLE DYSFUNCTION AND NECROSIS (DEATH)

In normal activity:

A nerve impulse ➡ alpha motor neurone travels ➡ cell membrane

Excitation – contraction occurs ➡ release of calcium ions (Ca)

Ca exert an action on the myofibrils ➡

CONTRACTION

In abnormal activity:

Disruption of Ca metabolism in muscle ➡

Muscle dysfunction and necrosis

Theory for this effect

Myopathy as a result of increased Ca influx

HYPERCONTRACTION of muscle fibre
= accumulation of LACTIC ACID ➡ Cell necrosis

GLOSSARY OF TERMS:
Myopathy: Any disease of the muscles. Usually with weakness and wasting plus pain and tenderness.
Myofibrils: One of numerous contractile filaments within muscle cells.

CAUSES OF MUSCLE MYOPATHIES

The main causes of myopathies include azoturia; electrolyte imbalance; hormone levels, particularly in fillies; and viral infections.

EXERCISE-INDUCED MYOPATHIES

Most myopathies are related to exercise, it being an initiating factor in most cases. Muscle is easily stressed, so a progressive exercise programme should be followed. Muscle damage can be detected in blood plasma by an increase in cell enzymes.

EXERTIONAL RHABDOMYOLYSIS (AZOTURIA)

Known as 'tying up', this affects the type II muscle fibres involving anaerobic metabolism, and therefore occurs as a result of fastwork exercise.

Many muscle problems in performance horses are the result of simple problems, and attention to management can very often bring about a cure. Thus observe the following:

- Avoid changing the feed suddenly before a competition.
- Ensure an adequate supply of hay for adequate potassium (k) levels.
- Supply salt in the daily diet, and supplement electrolytes in hot, humid weather or during prolonged activity.
- Older horses tend to stop drinking whilst on the move, especially when competing, so careful monitoring of intake and output is required.
- Make sure to follow 'correct' cooling methods when exercising in the heat or if the horse becomes hot:

    allow evaporation from the body (do not cover);
    apply masses of cold water to the hindquarters;
    sweat-scrape off the warm water;
    keep him moving, and moving the washing areas so he stays relaxed.

Signs of exertional myopathies:

- Gait abnormalities – stiff or stilted;
- elevated heart and respiratory rates due to pain;
- body temperature is increased due to muscle contraction;
- palpation of back and hindquarter muscles may be painful.

The symptoms of laminitis and tetanus may resemble 'tying up'.

Correct cooling of the muscles is important during and after strenuous exercise

Electrolyte Imbalance

In prolonged endurance competitions the horse can lose 25–50 litres of fluid; this results in a severe reduction in muscular capacity.

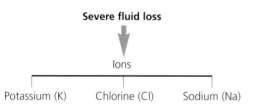

Severe fluid loss

Ions

Potassium (K)   Chlorine (Cl)   Sodium (Na)

These ions are important for neuromuscular function.

Example 1: If calcium (Ca) and magnesium (Mg) decrease, the result is an increase in nervousness and muscular twitching.

Example 2: If sodium (Na) and potassium (K) decrease, neuromuscular twitching decreases and also performance.

Prevention
On endurance rides, ensure the horse drinks water – but not cold, as this can cause colic.

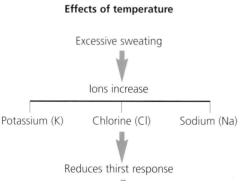

Effects of temperature

Excessive sweating

Ions increase

Potassium (K)   Chlorine (Cl)   Sodium (Na)

Reduces thirst response

Further dehydration

Prevention lies in the oral replacement of these electrolytes.

KEY POINT: Electrolytes may be added to the drinking water and squirted into the mouth. If they are put into a bucket, provide an alternative source of drinking water.

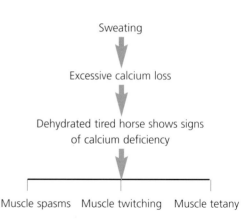

Sweating

Excessive calcium loss

Dehydrated tired horse shows signs of calcium deficiency

Muscle spasms   Muscle twitching   Muscle tetany

The longer the duration of the exercise and the higher the temperature and humidity, the greater the electrolyte loss. It therefore becomes more necessary to replace the electrolytes.

KEY POINT: Each horse is unique, so some are more susceptible to electrolyte imbalances than others.

Hormones

Individual hormone levels may affect muscular metabolism. Fillies are more prone to myopathies, especially if they are very anxious by nature. For example, thyroxine is involved in muscle oxidative metabolism and cellular processes. Hypothyroidism, due to a lack of thyroid, can cause stiffness of the gait and decreased endurance. The stress of training can induce hypothyroidism.

Viral Infections

Viral infections will also have a knock-on effect on the muscle function of the horse if he is stressed. This is particularly evident if the horse is worked during a flu episode, or has been returned to work too quickly following it.

KEY POINT: Always seek professional nutritional advice in the treatment of myopathies.

LABORATORY TESTS IN THE DIAGNOSIS OF MUSCLE DISEASE

Excessive contraction of muscles plus oxygen depletion results in muscle damage.

Blood serum checks	Normal levels*	
Lactase dehydrogenase (LDH)	383-664	
Creatine phosphokinase (CPK)	154-270 iu/1	10th–90th percentiles
Aspartate amino transferase (AST)	256-369 iu/1	

- All these increase in blood serum *normally* in horses in training.
- If all these enzymes are taken together, an increase can be an aid in the diagnosis and prognosis of muscle disease.
- The serum enzyme values correlate with the degree of muscle damage.

Enzyme	IU/L	Result
High CPK High AST	> 20,000 to 50,000	Severe muscle damage
Lower CPK Lower AST	1,000 to 2,000	Mild muscle inflammation Chronic muscle damage

Enzyme Level	Period of Injury
Increased CPK No increase AST or LDH	Acute muscle cell degeneration within past 6–12 hours
Increased CPK & LDH No increase AST	Acute muscle damage in last 24 hours
Increase AST & LDH No increase CPK	Muscle damage occurred 3 to 4 days before measurement

Serum electrolyte values
- Used for determining electrolyte role.
- Urine values on same day also taken.

This results in a calculation of the renal indices and fractional excretion of serum electrolytes.
The presence of myoglobin in the urine, causing a coffee colour, also indicates muscle damage.

Estimation of fluid loss
Packed cell volume (PCV) and total plasma protein in the blood is measured.

* Source of Normal levels: Beaufort Cottage Lab

> **GLOSSARY OF TERMS:**
> **Myoglobin:** Oxygen-carrying pigment of muscle

Management of Acute Myopathies
- Avoid movement.
- If hot, decrease temperature.
- Replace loss of fluids and electrolytes.
- Provide pain relief.
- Veterinary diagnosis to prevent further episodes.

Long Term
- Assess management.
- Assess nutritional input.

Management
- Exercise levels – progression, warming up.
- Fitness – avoid fatigue and assess ability to do the job.
- Diet – seek nutritional advice.
- Eliminate pain – if lame or neuromuscular dysfunction can be related.
- Reduce stress and anxiety.
- There is an increased risk in fillies.

Diagnosis
Diagnostic ultrasound will identify tissue damage.

Treatment and Care
In the acute stage:

- Cold therapy to reduce swelling.
- Immobilisation of the affected area for the first 24–48 hours to control the haemorrhaging.
- Use of electrotherapy to encourage removal of inflammatory exudates; example – pulsed shortwave therapy.

Also muscle manipulation to relax muscle spasm in minor cases.

In the sub-acute stage:
- Soft tissue mobilisations.
- Muscle stimulation.
- Electrotherapy.

When chronic:
- Restoration of normal range of motion by increasing flexibility and strength.
- Active and passive movements.
- Soft tissue mobilisations.

If the nerve is involved, the maintenance of muscle nutrition by active contraction of the muscle fibres is required until the nerve is functioning normally. This can be achieved using a neuromuscular stimulator. All muscle fibre types must be stimulated.

This horse is at full stretch. If he is fatigued, or twists and catches his hindlimbs on the fence, the chances are he will cause soft tissue injuries

Nerves

The nervous system comprises the central nervous system and the peripheral nervous system. Nerves are important for communication, and if they are damaged there can be serious consequences. They are very susceptible to pressure and temperature; if a nerve is damaged it will lead to atrophy of the muscle it feeds – that is, a breakdown in communication. Nerves that are myelinated can regenerate at a rate of 1mm per day. The pain sensation that nerves supply can be used as a diagnostic tool of lameness examinations.

GLOSSARY OF TERMS:
Myelination: Process in which myelin, a protective sheath, is laid around nerve fibres in the central or peripheral nervous systems.
Demyelination: A disease process damaging the myelin sheaths. This in turn affects the function of the nerve fibres which the myelin normally supports.

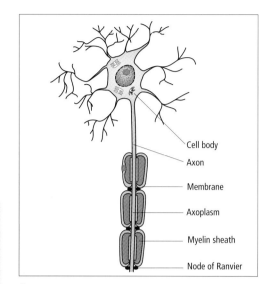

A nerve

Cell body
Axon
Membrane
Axoplasm
Myelin sheath
Node of Ranvier

DIAGNOSIS OF NERVE INJURIES

Electrophysiological techniques may be of value in assessing the severity of a lesion:
1 EMG;
2 motor and sensory nerve conduction studies plus muscle-evoked action potentials.

NERVE INJURIES

There are several types of nerve damage; those that are likely to be encountered by the horse owner are included here.

Neuropraxia

This condition involves compression, oedema and local demyelination, resulting in a complete block of impulse conduction in the nerve.

This is the mildest form of injury, with recovery usually occurring within one to two weeks, once the compression and oedema resolve. The local demyelination may take a little longer to reverse (about four to six weeks).

Axonotmesis

If the injury is more severe than that described above, the axon may degenerate distal to the lesion, but the axon sheaths remain intact.

Recovery will now depend on re-growth of the axons from the site of injury, which normally occurs no faster than 1–2mm per day.

Neurotmesis

This is the most severe form of nerve damage, with the loss not only of axonal continuity, but also of continuity of the whole nerve trunk. Regeneration is often incomplete.

Sweeny or Suprascapular Nerve Paralysis

This condition is due to damage to the affected nerve. It can be caused by partial pressure, or it can be due to degeneration of the axons.

The nerve covers the front of the scapula and can be damaged if the horse falls on the shoulder, receives a kick, or runs into something. It supplies two muscles:
• the supraspinatus muscle;
• the infraspinatus muscle.

In the acute stage, the aims of management are:
• to reduce swelling if evident;
• to assist the inflammatory process;
• to maintain muscle nutrition, and contractibility of the muscle;

61

- to aid circulation and venous/lymphatic drainage;
- to address the effects of injury on the rest of the body; if it were caused by a fall, to assess spinal mobility;
- care of foot balance, as often the weight is transferred across to the good side.

The methods used to achieve the aims described above are:
- Ultrasound/laser/cold therapy (though careful monitoring is necessary if treatment includes cold therapy, due to the decreased sensation).

- Neurotrophic stimulation to assist muscle pump and blood supply.
- Maintaining the base-line support of the postural muscle fibres. These are the slow-twitch, red, oxidative muscle fibres.
- Massage and muscle stimulation.
- Spinal mobilisation and massage.
- Regular foot trimming.

Atrophy of the shoulder muscles from nerve damage to the suprascapular nerve

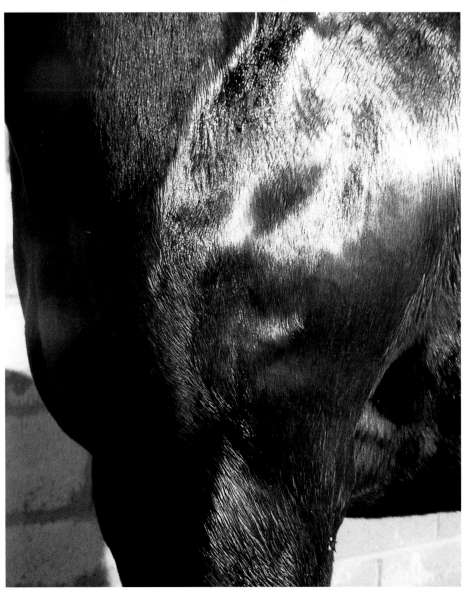

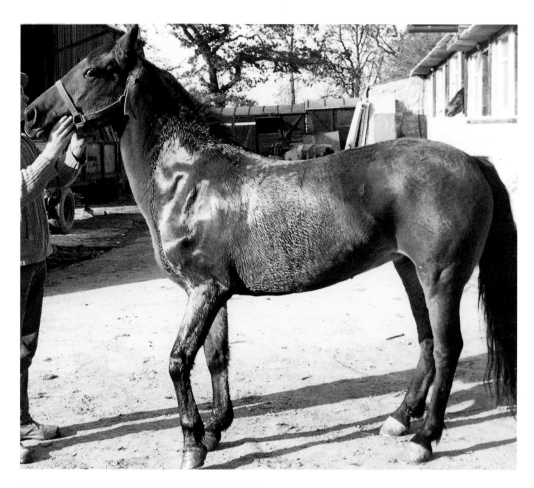

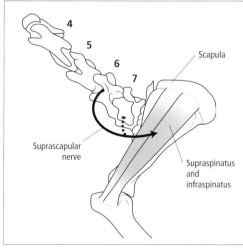

Skeletal diagram showing the radial nerve, C567 nerve roots and scapular innervation

Radial nerve paralysis. The muscles which extend the elbow, knee and hoof are non-functional so all the joints are held flexed, with the elbow dropped.

Radial Nerve Paralysis

The muscles that extend to the elbow, knee and hoof will be affected. Damage normally occurs where it passes around the humerus, and can be the result of a knock or fall.

Signs/Symptoms

The horse cannot move the leg forwards properly, and as a result will drag the toe. He tries to cope by swinging the leg outwards as it is advanced.

Treatment

- Rest, to allow the nerve to recover.
- Muscle stimulation.

The Spine

CONDITIONS OF THE NECK

ACUTE NECK PAIN

Signs/Symptoms

- Localised swelling.
- Unable to lower or raise the head above a certain height.
- Localised sweating.
- Localised, small muscle contractions.
- Problems chewing (TMJ joints).
- Stiffness of the neck.
- Straddling the forelimbs, or going down on one knee to graze.

Causes

If the onset of these symptoms is sudden, then the cause may be directly related to a fall, or some sort of dramatic trauma. Otherwise the horse's problems may be attributed to the following type of risk factor:

- getting his head stuck through a fence;
- catching his headcollar or bridle on a fixed object;
- going over backwards;

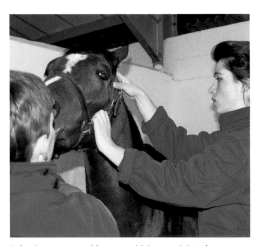

Palpation may reveal hypersensitivity over joints, bones or soft tissues in the neck

- banging his head on a door frame, or similar.

The signs/symptoms indicative of the sub-acute stage are:

- head tilt;
- head shaking;
- resentment of being bridled or handled around the head;
- dislike of being ridden, and particularly being mounted.

The signs/symptoms indicative of the chronic stage are:

- head tilt;
- muscular atrophy;
- stiffness one way;
- abnormal posture;
- abnormal muscle development: the muscles across the forehead/hypertrophy of the temporal muscle and/or the splenius muscle;
- abnormal sensitivity over the atlas (where the headpiece sits);
- change of gait;
- hopping into trot;
- abnormal movement of neck, known as 'fowl' neck – moving it like a chicken;
- inability to rein back;

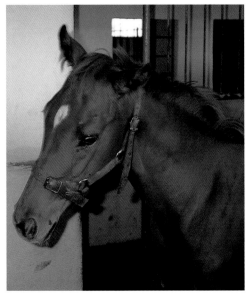

This foal had a neck vertebrae fracture with a resultant head tilt and nerve damage

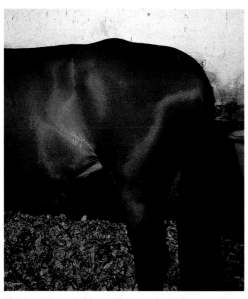

This horse has a visible swelling over the midline sacroiliac area

- inability to laterally flex neck without trick movements on short turns around you (right and left);
- not accepting the bit;
- sore thoracic lumbar region;
- localised swelling.

Treatment
- Acute stage
The aims of treatment in the acute stage are to reduce excessive inflammatory response, and to control pain. The methods to do so include ice, electrotherapy and acupuncture.

- Sub-acute stage
In the sub-acute stage they are to maintain pain-free range of motion, to aid correct healing, and to control pain. The methods to do so include muscle stimulation, massage, and soft tissue mobilisation/manipulation (such as physiotherapy, chiropractic).

- Chronic stage
In this stage it is hoped to restore normal movement patterns. The methods to do so include osteopathy under sedation/general anaesthetic; and physiotherapy – stretching, mobilising, and adjusting any muscle imbalance.

THORACOLUMBAR SPINE
General Signs/Symptoms
- Muscle guarding
- Stiffness
- Change of posture

The symptoms indicative of the acute stage are:

- rearing;
- refusing to go forwards;
- problems going down hill;
- 'cold backed' when first ridden;
- bucking on transition to canter;
- muscle spasms;
- swelling.

The symptoms indicative of the chronic stage are:

- decreased flexibility on circle;
- poor shape over fences;
- rushing fences;
- poor muscling.

Causes
The predisposing feature for this condition could be changes to the dorsal spinous processes so that they override or impinge on each other (known as 'kissing spines'). This causes inflammation and possibly structural changes. It is more common in the mid-back region and in short-backed horses,

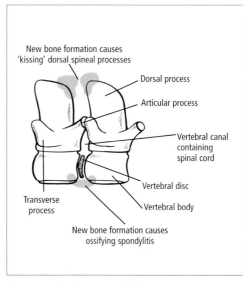

Dorsal spine impingement or 'kissing' spines

Bucking can be due to naughtiness, fear, resentment or pain

especially thoroughbreds. It is worth noting that on post mortem, a great many horses show these findings, but have not had a dorsal spinal impingement problem identified whilst working.

A symptom of this condition is that on reflex testing the horse is reluctant to dip and arch his back. He will tend to hold it rigidly, with the muscles protectively guarding the spine.

If he is badly affected he will be reluctant to carry a rider – he may rear, buck, or refuse to go forwards; in a less severe case he will be resentful of the saddle, and show considerable sensitivity along the back.

KEY POINT: A great many of these horses do appear to have had a trigger such as a fall or a faulty saddle, which would exacerbate the clinical signs.

Diagnosis
Local anaesthetic is used to desensitise the area, and the horse is then ridden to see if there is any favourable change in his behaviour. Gamma scintigraphy can be used to identify any active inflammatory process, and then radiography to confirm the diagnosis. Note that although there may be signs of changes on x-rays, clinically the horse may not feel pain in the area. It is important to distinguish this.

Treatment
- Some horses respond to rest, combined with complementary therapies.
- Cortisone may be injected into the affected area, and the horse then worked.
- Phenylbutazone can be prescribed to allow the horse to relax and work.
- In certain cases the summits of the offending dorsal spinous processes are removed, but this requires specialised surgery.

Complementary therapies can be used to treat horses with dorsal spinous impingement; such treatment would aim to:

- relieve muscle spasm;
- improve the range of motion of the affected area;
- identify postural changes;
- correct the biomechanics and so relieve the problem area.

These therapies might include:

- acupuncture, to relieve pain and facilitate normal movement;
- osteopathy under sedation, to 're-programme' and provide a normal neural patterning to allow functional movement;
- physiotherapy, to desensitise, and damp down pain signals to effect normal muscle and nerve responses. Also to correct muscle imbalances, and rehabilitate movement patterns to enable correct neuromotor firing sequences.

SPRAIN OF THE SUPRASPINOUS LIGAMENT
Causes
- Falling at high speed.
- Damage to back from impact when going over backwards.
- Rolling on a stone.

Signs/Symptoms
- Localised inflammation.
- Bucking, particularly if the saddle slips to one side. This often happens because of the muscle atrophy that results, causing an imbalance.
- Restricted movement.

Diagnosis/Treatment
- Diagnostic ultrasound and radiography.
- Rest combined with physiotherapy to stimulate healing and prevent secondary problems.
- Osteopathy under sedation.
- Physiotherapy/chiropractic to correct the musculoskeletal dysfunction that resulted from the fall.

KEY POINT: These cases can take a long time to heal. Correct saddle fit is vital.

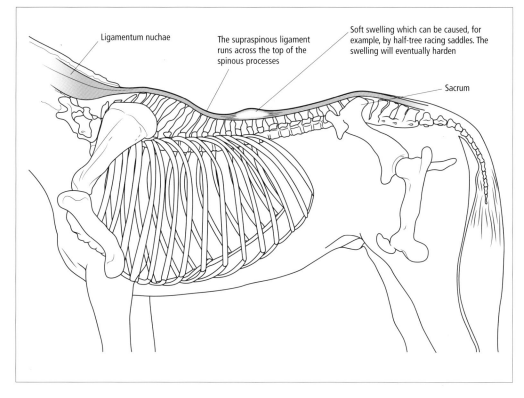

Ligamentum nuchae

The supraspinous ligament runs across the top of the spinous processes

Soft swelling which can be caused, for example, by half-tree racing saddles. The swelling will eventually harden

Sacrum

FRACTURE OF THE WITHERS

Cause

- The withers can be fractured if the horse rears over backwards.

Signs

- There will be swelling and crepitus over the area.

Diagnosis

- Radiography is the usual method of diagnosis.

> **GLOSSARY OF TERMS:**
> **Crepitus:** Crackling sound and grating feeling under the skin.

Treatment

In the acute stage of the condition treatment would aim to:

- resolve the swelling;
- relieve pain;
- correct musculoskeletal dysfunction.

A made-to-measure saddle may be required so as to ensure a correct fit. Rugs may also be a problem initially, if they cause pressure on the wither area. Nevertheless, the prognosis is normally very good.

STRAIN OF THE SACROILIAC JOINT

The sacrum, consisting of five fused vertebrae, is joined to the ileum to form the sacroiliac joint. The bones of particular significance in this structure are the tuber sacrale, the tuber coxae and the ischial tuberosity. These are joined by three ligaments known as the dorsal sacroiliac, the lateral sacroiliac and the sacro sciatic.

The muscles involved are the gluteals, the iliopsoas, the quadriceps, the hamstrings, and the tensor fascia lata. Their function is to transmit forces from the spine to the lower extremities, and vice versa, along with the dampening and distribution of ground reaction forces during gait.

The causes of dysfunction might include falls, slipping, twisting or high stress to the sacroiliac joint, or repeated trauma.

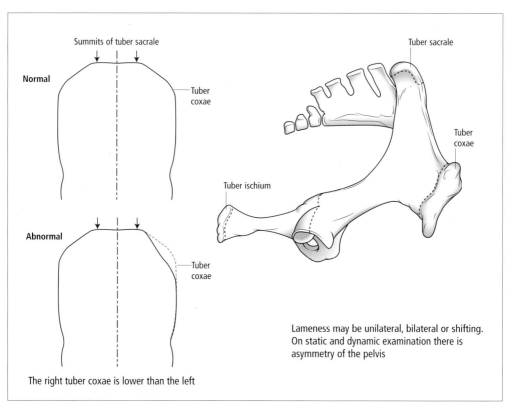

Summits of tuber sacrale

Normal

Tuber coxae

Tuber sacrale

Tuber coxae

Abnormal

Tuber coxae

Tuber ischium

Lameness may be unilateral, bilateral or shifting. On static and dynamic examination there is asymmetry of the pelvis

The right tuber coxae is lower than the left

Signs/Symptoms
- Not working straight.
- Refusing the correct canter lead.
- Difficulty turning short, and crossing the back legs over.
- Low back and gluteal muscle pain.
- Lack of impulsion.
- Dislike of lifting the hind limbs (often the opposite leg to the one affected).

Asymmetry of the tuber sacrale may be due to:

- partial dislocation of the sacroiliac joint;
- bone malformation;
- muscle atrophy;
- old pelvic fracture.

Diagnosis
All other causes of lameness should be eliminated. This is a very difficult area to radiograph, and is normally only possible with the horse on its back under general anaesthetic. Gamma scintigraphy (p34) is more commonly used to identify damage, and ultrasonograpy (p33) to diagnose muscle and ligament trauma.

Prognosis
Some horses remain stiff and have a low grade lameness; however, this appears to be due to a mechanical instability of the joints, rather than to pain. Good musculature and the correction of any muscle imbalances enable a good functional return. Long periods of rest are not advocated due to the instability caused by muscle disease. In the chronic stage, it may be of benefit to turn the horse out in a field with a hill to maintain muscle bulk.

In the acute stages, it will help the horse's balance to shoe him on a good surface against a wall. This may be a long-term problem due to a loss of confidence through feeling unstable on three legs.

Rehabilitation may be attempted using the Monty Roberts' method, TTEAM and Parelli; these horsemanship skills help to develop confidence and mobility by enhancing sensory and motor skills and movement awareness.

TREATMENT

	Aims	Methods
Acute	Reduce pain Assist healing Maintain nutrition	Cold therapy, electrotherapy, acupuncture Muscle stimulation
Sub-acute	Restore muscle symmetry and pelvis mobility Assist healing	Mobilisation, manipulation Electrotherapy
Chronic	Stimulate normal function Strengthen mobility	Rehabilitation Muscle stimulation Manipulation Suppling exercises

Summary of Veterinary Disease and Lameness

Signs	Cause
Forelimb lameness with no obvious focus of pain or swelling	Foot pain Early degenerative disease High suspensory desmitis Subchondral bone cyst OCD lesion
Stumbling	Tiredness – fatigue Poor terrain Poor foot balance Foot pain Incoordination Upper neck pain Musculoskeletal dysfunction (back)
Hind limb lameness with no obvious focus of pain or swelling	Unfit Laziness/poor riding Poor foot balance Bone spavin developing Pelvic problems Musculoskeletal dysfunction
Hind limb toe drag	Bone spavin Subchondral bone cyst High suspensory desmitis Early degenerative joint disease
Very severe lameness	Nerve damage so unable to bear weight Foot abscess Fracture Joint infection
Poor performance	Reproductive system – ovaries Respiratory problem Metabolic disorder – anaemia Bilateral forelimb lameness Bilateral hindlimb lameness
Behavioural	Teeth Dorsal spinous impingement Musculoskeletal dysfunction Foot pain Inadequate training Badly fitting tack

GLOSSARY OF TERMS:
Desmitis: Inflammation
OCD: Osteochondritis dissecans, developmental abnormality of cartilage and bone

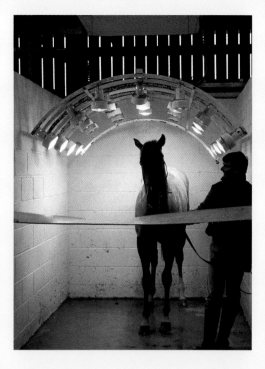

The Use of Cold and Heat in Treatment

Both heat and cold have their place in the treatment of the injured horse. Both appear to be useful in relieving pain and muscle spasm, though each has a somewhat different role. Thus recent trauma benefits from immediate cooling, which will reduce the bleeding, the rate of swelling and the pain; yet later that same injury (after 48 hours) will benefit from mild heating, to increase metabolism and gently increase healing pressures. Indeed, cold has been shown to diminish healing at this later stage. Joint stiffness is improved by heating and made worse by cooling; conversely heat will encourage swelling, whereas cold will help to control it.

The Use of Cold Therapy

Cold therapy, or cryotherapy, refers to the therapeutic use of local or general body cooling. Cooling is the transfer of heat energy away from the body tissues: the result is to lower the local tissue temperature and provoke the body into regulating the body heat. The vast majority of cold treatments are given with crushed ice, so heat is transferred by conduction from the skin; the energy generated is used in changing the state of the substance from a solid to a liquid – in this case by melting the ice.

In recent injury, cooling has several uses:

• If the wound is bleeding, it serves to promote immediate vasoconstriction.
• Prompt cooling lowers the tissue temperature and limits tissue damage (although it must not be too intense or prolonged, as it may then delay blood coagulation).
• It diminishes the rate of swelling and the production of irritants.
• In the early stages of injury (during the initial two hours) it will minimise secondary cell necrosis by reducing the metabolic rate.
• It can lessen the inflammatory reaction.

Pain is also reduced by cold, inasmuch as if the swelling is reduced, then so is the pressure. Furthermore fewer pain-inducing irritants will be released; and there will be a direct effect on the conduction of pain receptors and neurons. Thus cold affects the pain gate mechanism (see page 16), and the release of endorphins and encephalins (natural pain killers). Muscle spasm – a vicious circle of muscle guarding – is curtailed by the application of cold, which then allows an increased range of motion.

Finally, cold is used in chronic inflammation and effusion, and in muscle strengthening and stretching.

METHODS OF APPLYING COLD THERAPY

Cold therapy involves cooling the body surface by applying a substance to the surface that is at a lower temperature, so cooling by conduction.

Buckets of cold water and ice ready to be used at a horse trials.Cooling the muscles after exertion is vital to return the body temperature to normal

Local Immersion

This method is suitable for treating an injury to the foot or lower leg. The leg is placed in a suitable high-sided rubber bin or bucket (or a purpose-made jacuzzi boot), then cold water and ice added. An ideal temperature is around 16–18°C, and the leg immersed for fifteen to twenty minutes. Agitate the water around the limb to disperse any warming-up effect, and add more ice if necessary.

Cold Packs

Crush the ice and place in a wet towel or in a towelling bag, and place on the skin. The water will warm up, so re-saturate the towel pack with cold water during the treatment to prevent this.

WARNING: BE SURE TO MONITOR THE SKIN FOR DAMAGE FROM ICE BURN.

Another useful way of applying ice to a horse's leg is to double over a piece of 'tubigrip' and place crushed ice between; again, it is advisable to periodically saturate the tubigrip with cold water. Apply for ten minutes.

Commercial Cold Packs

These come in various sizes and are normally stored in the fridge, therefore at temperatures below 10°C; however, this is more likely to be around –5°C, or even –12°C. So initially these packs are at a lower temperature than ordinary ice packs, and therefore have the potential to cool the skin very rapidly. However, once in place their temperature will inevitably rise swiftly. They should be placed over a wet towel to prevent burns, and left in situ for ten minutes.

Ice Massage Applications

The theory of massage therapy is that its counter-irritant action will relieve pain. It will also help to

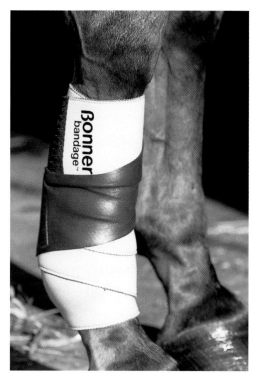
Various commerical cold boots or bandages are available

stimulate the muscles by briefly stimulating the areas of skin supplied by the same nerve roots as those of the muscle.

For massage, use an ice cube either wrapped in a cloth, or as an ice 'lollipop' on a wooden stick. Move the ice block over the part using a slow, circular motion, for some minutes.

For muscle stimulation the ice should be applied only briefly, either dabbing for about four seconds at a time, or by using short strokes applied over the skin.

THE RISKS INHERENT IN COLD THERAPY

- Excessive local cold can damage normal tissue.
- Some pathological conditions may predispose the patient to injury as a result of cold treatment; thus they may succomb to temperature falls that would otherwise be harmless.
- If autonomic nerves are affected, tissue cooling occurs more rapidly and more deeply than normal. Therefore caution is required if skin with defective innervation is to be treated.

Applying astringent clay is a quick method of cooling legs

The Therapeutic Uses of Superficial Heating

The use of heat on an injured part has four main effects: it relieves pain, it has a sedative effect, it encourages healing, and it helps to increase the range of motion.

- Pain relief, because sensory receptors activate the pain gate mechanism (see page 12).
- A sedative effect, because it helps to decrease muscle spasm.
- Encourages healing, because mild inflammation benefits from a temperature rise between 2 and 5°C: it causes an increase in the action of healing blood cells, and similarly an increase in the absorption of exudate.

Heat can be applied in various ways, from one lamp directed by hand (as below) or by the more sophisticated arrangement of a specially set-up box

- An increase in the range of motion, for three main reasons:
  1 Heat has an analgesic effect, and so it encourages a greater tolerance to stretching.
  2 The viscosity of the tissues is reduced, so there is a corresponding reduction in joint stiffness.
  3 Heat increases the elasticity of scar tissue, so it is used prior to passive stretching and/or exercise to increase joint movement in order to lengthen scars or contracted tissue.

METHODS OF APPLYING HEAT
Hot Packs

The use of commercially available heat packs is common; however, if you choose these it is important to ensure that there is some interface between the skin and the pack. Otherwise, heat

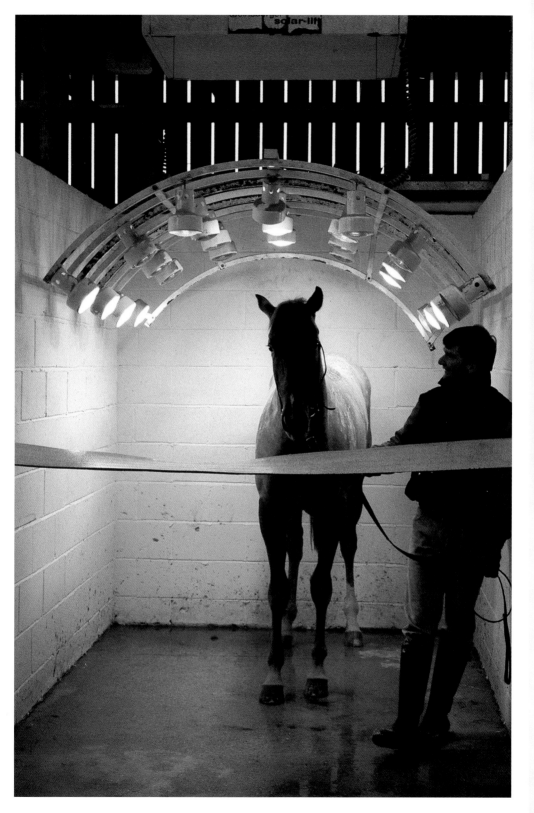

can be applied using partially filled hot water bottles covered in a protective towel. Hand-held massagers sometimes have a heat component.

Apply heat for 10–15 minutes, and always check for discomfort or skin damage.

Infrared (IR)

Radiation in the electromagnetic spectrum will be absorbed by the body as heat, if the wavelengths fall within the visible band from 7,700A units, to the shortwave bands at the 45Mc range. The absorption of infrared (7,700 to 120,000A units) will take place within the top 3mm of tissues. There are two types of unit: luminous units that emit infrared from glowing bulbs; and non-luminous units that rely on a non-glowing source.

What is infrared used for?
• To increase the circulation.
• Because it has a sedative effect on superficial nerve endings.
• To lower blood pressure.

When is it used?
• In cases of mild or chronic pain.
• To help improve circulatory conditions.
• As an adjunct therapy, for instance, before mobilisation exercises to relax and prepare for treatment.

Treatment procedures
Place non-luminous lamps directly over the target areas at a distance of 24–36in (60–90cm). Areas to be treated on the legs and body should be targeted for 10 to 30min; on the face, the head and the neck it should be for a shorter duration, 10–15min.

Luminous lamps should be positioned at a distance of 30–42in (75–105cm) and at an angle of 45°. Note that luminous lamps often feel hotter superficially.

The risks inherent in infrared treatment
Take care against burns: the horse could risk incurring a burn if it moves too close to the light source and actually touches the lights whilst it is being treated. Take care, particularly if there is metal on the head collar, that there is no chance of the horse getting too close to the light source. You should also check the horse's skin before, during and after treatment.

Finally, before treatment is started, check that the horse is not wearing a combustible rug.

Infrared should not be used at all in the following circumstances:

• Where there is skin irritation: most acute inflammatory skin conditions are made worse by heating. Also, some chemical irritants on the skin have their effects increased by heating, and this leads to irritation or inflammation. Be sure to remove all liniments prior to treatment.
• In acute febrile illness (fever): particular care should be taken when the horse's heat regulation system is under stress.
• Where there are tumours of the skin, as these may be stimulated.

HOT AND COLD SUMMARY

Both heat and cold appear to be useful in relieving pain and muscle spasm. Thus, recent trauma benefits from immediate cooling to reduce bleeding, the rate of swelling, and pain. Later, however, the same injury (after 48 hours) will benefit from mild heating to increase metabolism and gently increase healing pressures. Cold has been shown to diminish healing.

Any swelling tends to be encouraged by heat, but decreased by cooling. Cooling impairs skilled movements, reduces spasticity, and facilitates muscle activity.

Joint stiffness is decreased by heating, and increased by cooling.

Electrotherapy and its Success in Treatment

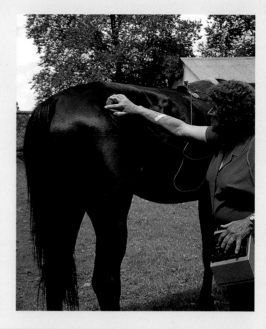

When electromodalities are used in the treatment of the horse it is essential that respect be paid to the electrical nature of their body. The vast neurological network within the body dwarfs NASA when it comes to circuitry, and has an abundance of complex ionic exchangers. An appreciation of the body's electrophysiology and the electrical qualities of the modality of choice is essential for appropriate treatment; these modalities might include ultrasound; magnetic and electromagnetic therapies; TENS (transcutaneous electrical stimulation); and laser therapy. As the body functions by electricity, its malfunction can also be measured by using electricity, namely with an electrocardiogram (ECG) or an electromyogram (EMG). Most forms of therapeutic electrotherapy are quite old. Among the 'newer' modalities is the cold laser.

Current veterinary practice is also now aware of the concept of endorphins, the role they play in pain control, and how horses, like ourselves, can produce B-endorphins. Pain normally triggers the production of this chemical, which provides an analgesic effect and can be further enriched by the use of electrical currents to the surface of the body. This is also achieved by the use of manual therapy, namely acupressure, massage and healing. As far as the veterinary surgeon or the physiotherapist is concerned, the key to successful practice in electrotherapy is a working knowledge of the basic physics of each modality, and knowing which to select at which stages of recovery.

Thus for electrotherapy treatment to be effective, it is important to:

- select the modality skilfully;
- administer effective treatment;
- adapt appropriately when necessary;
- evaluate the results accurately.

Ultrasound Therapy

HOW IT WORKS

Ultrasound (u/s) refers to mechanical vibrations that are essentially the same as sound waves, but of a higher frequency. Therapeutic ultrasound therapy gives pulsated heat, and the micromassage thereby produced is particularly useful in tendon and muscle injuries. Incorrect technique will lead to negative therapeutic effects: thus high continuous intensities result in high pressure and temperature changes, and therefore gross tissue damage. Also, standing waves are caused by the poor technique of not moving the transducer head during treatment.

HOW TO APPLY IT

In the first instance, treatment will almost certainly be administered by the veterinary surgeon, or by the physiotherapist or professional body. Units for 'home' administration should only be considered and used having obtained professional advice and guidance.

- The hair may be clipped – and if so, clipping should be repeated regularly – or gel can be laid down on top of the hair (although there has been no research on the effects of energy absorption of pulsed, low intensity ultrasound on animals with hair).
- A couplant must be placed between the area to be treated and the head of the u/s; this can be water, or a plastic glove filled with water, or a gel suitable for ultrasound transmission. (Never turn the machine on without the couplant or water contact on the ultrasound head, as the transducer will be damaged by the reflected beam.) Unless the operators' manual indicates otherwise.
- Always run a test to check if the ultrasound is working. Use a water bath, and reflect an

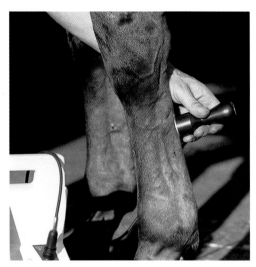

Ultrasound is used for tendon and ligament injuries and inflammation

ultrasonic beam up to the surface, where it should produce ripples.
- The movement of the ultrasound head is very important for effective treatment. In order not to cause damage to the tissue, this should be slow and continuous, using circles or overlapping series of parallel lines.
- Inherent risks: 'hot spots' can develop if not irradiated properly.

THE EFFECTS OF ULTRASOUND ON INJURED TISSUE

At the acute stage ultrasound treatment will:
- increase the release of histamine and growth factors, which will speed up the healing process;
- accelerate the normal resolution of inflammation.

At the granulation stage it will:
- stimulate collagen synthesis, and the resulting collagen will have increased tensile strength;
- encourage the growth of those cells that fight infection and regulate inflammation;
- encourage the growth of new capillaries in tissue that is chronically deficient in blood.

At the remodelling stage it will:
- improve the straight alignment of mature collagen, as in scar tissue;

CAUTION

Do not use an ultrasound machine without a chartered physiotherapist (UK) or physical therapist (USA) checking the apparatus and giving treatment guidelines. This equipment, if used incorrectly, can aggravate tissue repair and cause pain.

ULTRASOUND MECHANISMS

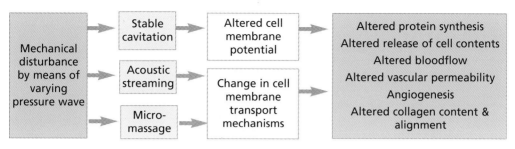

GLOSSARY OF TERMS
Angiogenesis: Growth of new blood vessels.

- promote the re-orientation of fibres, which leads to greater elasticity;
- relieve pain.

WHEN TO USE ULTRASOUND

Conditions that would be suitable for the use of ultrasound include:
- soft tissue sports injuries;
- surgical wounds;
- chronic arthritis conditions;
- circulatory conditions, such as ulcers;
- scar tissue.

It would not be suitable to use an ultrasound scanner over tumours, recent haemorrhaging, a pregnant uterus, or epiphyseal plates.

DANGERS OF ULTRASOUND

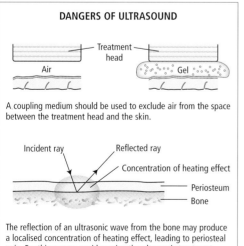

A coupling medium should be used to exclude air from the space between the treatment head and the skin.

The reflection of an ultrasonic wave from the bone may produce a localised concentration of heating effect, leading to periosteal pain. For this reason, avoid passing the ultrasonic treatment head over the subcutaneous bony points because it will cause pain and damage.

ULTRASOUND IMPROVES THE EFFICIENCY OF THE INFLAMMATORY PROCESS

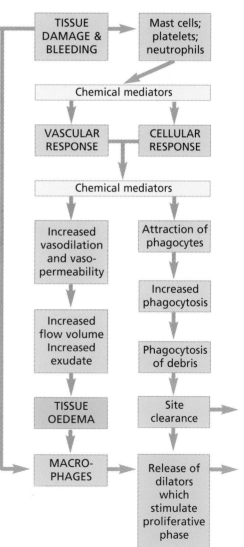

Magnetic and Electromagnetic Therapy

The effects of magnetic fields on the body tissues are complex, poorly understood and generally not well studied. Although there are no proven effects associated with the use of magnetic fields in horses, reported benefits may be related to the placebo effect or the heat generated under magnetic pads.

KEY POINTS:
- Pulsating electromagnetic field therapy, such as 'Magnetopulse', 'Respond' and 'Centurion', are not the same as static magnetic therapy.
- There are no established mechanisms of action to explain how either pulsating electromagnetic field or static magnetic field therapy could affect tissue.

The clinical effects of these two therapies in horses have not been documented.

Static magnetic rugs are widely used

STATIC MAGNETIC FIELD THERAPY

Static Magnetic Rugs

These rugs generate a continuous static magnetic influence on the targeted tissue, which cannot be altered. The magnets vary in their intensity from 500–14,000 gauss.

There are no guidelines on the length of time of application, or whether they should be applied in acute conditions.

If placed over an acute injury, the area sweats. It is therefore suggested that to avoid further haemorrhaging, they should not be used in acute conditions.

Most people apply them as boots, or inside pockets placed on the underside of the rug. Some magnets are placed at spinal nerve root level for purported pain relief effects.

TIPS:
- If you drop magnets you permanently damage them.
- As we do not fully understand their mechanism of action, on applying magnets for the first time, only do so under supervision and for a short period of time.

ELECTROMAGNETIC THERAPY

These low frequency, pulsed electromagnetic field therapy devices are normally lightweight, portable units that are designed to treat horses sometimes through blankets, as well as through plaster casts. They are normally simple to use, with a recipe book of possible applications varying the time, intensity and frequency. The correct placing of the applicators or the rug is all that is required, and then a battery pack or electrical socket. It allows a large area of the body and limbs to be treated at the same time.

How they work and produce their effects is not entirely known or understood. They are approved in the United States for humans for the treatment of delayed and non-union fractures. In one study for fresh fractures, healing was actually delayed when treated.

As yet there is no consensus on the optimal

variables, such as signal configuration and duration of treatment. However, anecdotally it has been reported to help loosen up horses prior to exercise, and to assist in pain relief in sacroiliac or pelvic injuries.

CARE OF EQUIPMENT

Have all leads, plugs and sockets inspected and checked for damage. Avoid trailing the leads in water, and have a circuit breaker in situ. Always place a muzzle on the horse if there is any possibility that he can reach the leads. Avoid excessive coiling of the leads after application, and always store the equipment at room temperature.

All physiotherapy machines need to be calibrated by electrical engineers, who specialise in this area (do this at least once a year). If your machine spends a lot of time being portable, then more frequent servicing is necessary.

Left and below: Electromagnetic therapy aids relaxation and appears to help stiffness.

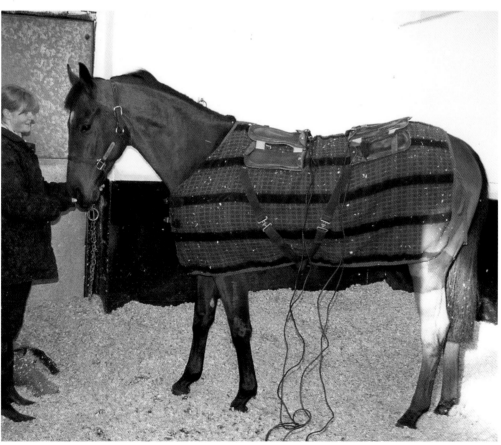

Electrical Massagers

On the market today there are various battery- and mains-supplied massagers. Some offer variable speeds of vibration and heat, some only massage. There are no research papers to provide rationale behind their application, but clinically the effects of pain relief and relaxation induced by these devices can be observed and explained via an understanding of the 'pain gate theory' (see page 12) and psychological factors.

The unit should be placed in situ and left for ten to forty minutes. The hand-held ones have to

THE EFFECTS OF MASSAGERS	
Effects	*Achieved by*
Psychological	Relaxation or decreased stress
Placebo	Owners feel they have done something
Warming up/down	Prevention of injuries and by increasing circulation and decreasing muscle soreness ie vasodilation effects
Decreasing muscle spasm	Pain gate or decreased stress
Reduction of pain	Pain gate

be moved over and through the tissues in order to have an effect.

A massager would not be useful if its application increased the patient's stress. Equally its use would be counter-productive where a heating effect is not wanted, for instance when there is haemorrhaging or an acute injury.

KEY POINTS:
- If a massager has not been used on your horse before, or if he dislikes clippers, take care when he is first treated with it. To begin with, place the pad on and do not turn the unit on.
- Use a numnah that offers protection to the spine to prevent pressure or heating from the components of the device.
- For your own safety, battery-driven packs are better because there is then no electric lead to get tangled up in.

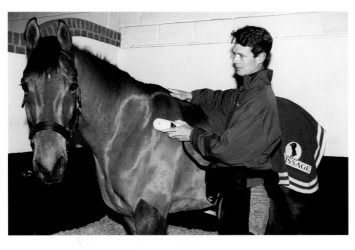

Equissage, a form of electrical massage performed before exercise to warm and relax tissues

The muscles around the girth and shoulder area benefit from massage before exercise. An increase in stride length has been reported

MUSCLE STIMULATORS

These stimulators deliver an electric signal that causes a muscle twitch, and are used for muscles whether the nerve supply is intact or damaged. If a muscle has been damaged by direct trauma or nerve interruption, then muscle stimulation is needed to maintain the blood circulation in, and the tone of, the muscle (trophism).

Where serious muscle atrophy has occurred, it is always important to stimulate the red muscle fibres (postural) initially in order to have a good base of support. This is essential for a functional muscle at the end of the day.

Muscles are composed of different fibre types, as shown in the table.

MUSCLE FIBRE TYPES		
Red muscle (Slow oxidative)	*Intermediate* (Fast oxidative)	*White muscle* (Fast twitch)
10pps	15pps	30–35pps
Postural	Glycolytic	Superficial

Faradic muscle stimulation was one way of delivering this treatment, but because it fires at 60pps, it is firing too high physiologically. It also

A neurotrophic stimulator is programmed to mimic normal muscle firing frequencies and can therefore be used for long periods of time

---

CAUTION

Do not use muscle stimulators where there is a fresh fracture for fear of causing unwanted motion in its proximity, or where there is active haemorrhage.

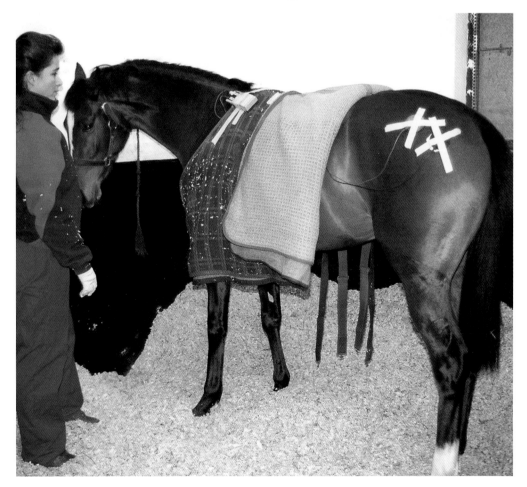

causes fatigue, and if done for more than 10 minutes on alternate days, it will cause muscle fibre damage.

KEY POINT: Always check the firing frequency of your muscle stimulator. Seek professional advice in order that appropriate stimulation is administered.

Circumstances that would be suitable for the use of a muscle stimulator include:

- the treatment of nerve injuries and muscle damage;
- in order to warm up muscles before exercise;
- in preparation for athletic endeavour, ie to increased joint awareness;
- for pain relief;
- re-education of movement;
- where there is muscle spasm;
- increase circulation.

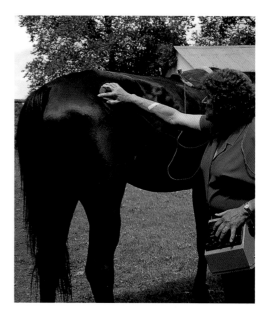

Muscle stimulators come in many guises; check your machine's parameters before deciding on how long to use it

TENS: Transcutaneous Electrical Stimulation

TENS is used primarily for pain relief; it can be used frequently, and almost anywhere on the horse. These units are relatively easy to apply, and are often bought and used by owners themselves once they have sought professional advice.

Settings on TENS
- Pain Gate Activation – 90-130Hz
- Opioid system activation – 2-5Hz

Electrode Placement
Target stimulus at:
- Appropriate spinal level
- Either side of lesion
- Over nerve roots
- Over peripheral nerve
- At motor points
- At trigger/acupuncture points
- Dermatome, Myotome, Sclerotome

CAUTION

When using any muscle stimulator, electrodes and gel must be applied to the skin. Care must be taken in preparing the skin both before treatment, and especially afterwards. Do not continue to treat if there is any sign of skin irritation.

Laser Therapy

'LASER' is an acronym for 'light amplification by stimulated emission of radiation': it is the production of a beam of radiation that differs from ordinary light.

HOW DOES IT WORK?
As can be seen in the diagram, there are different types of laser. Low power lasers cause no significant heating of the tissue. To have the best effect, lasers should be applied at right angles to, and in contact with, the surface. The penetration depth is considered to be a few millimetres, though different wavelengths have different penetration depths, the greatest being those in the near-infrared, such as 904nm. Skin lesions or superficial wound surfaces are treated appropriately by red lasers, i.e. 660nm, which will be absorbed largely in the skin.

HOW TO USE IT
Treatment involves a series of separate applications at select points, because of the narrow beam available. The cluster probe treats larger areas if required, and has varied wavelengths and both true laser and LED lights. In practice, treatment of wounds should not involve the laser touching the skin surface, to avoid wound disruption. Another option is to use probes that allow placement in holes or cavities. Conditions that are suitable for treatment include:

* for wound healing;
* in pain control;
* for acute and chronic soft tissue injuries:
    muscle spasm
    nerve inflammation
    arthritic conditions;
* in acupuncture or triggerpoint therapy;

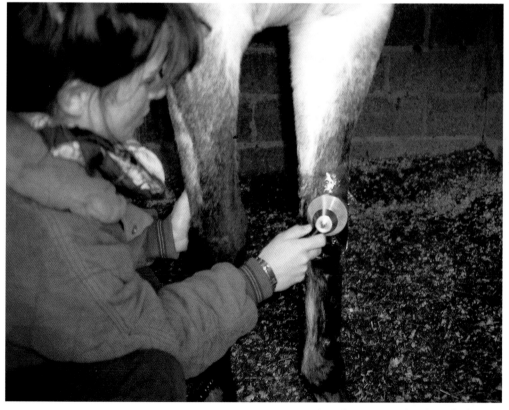

LASER is used to treat wounds and superficial injuries

CLASSIFICATION OF LASERS

Effect	Number	Range of power	Usage
No effect on eyes or skin	1	Low power	Blackboard printer
	2		Supermarket barcode reader
Safe on skin	3A	Mid-power	Therapeutic, also called low laser
	3B		
Unsafe on eyes and skin	4	High power	Surgical destructive

- during fracture consolidation;
- in post-traumatic nerve degeneration;
- where there is increased nerve conduction latency, producing an analgesic effect.

The effects of laser treatment will include:

- more organised fibroblasts (healing blood cells);
- increased cellularity;
- increased collagen formation;
- vasodilation;
- DNA synthesis;
- RNA production;
- pain gate.

Common Applications for Laser Therapy

In routine clinical practice, LASER is most commonly applied in problems such as:

- wound healing;
- pain relief;
- soft tissue injury;
- inflammatory arthropathies;
- laser acupuncture.

GLOSSARY OF TERMS
Arthropathy: Disease of a joint.

DOSAGE

There is a wide variation in recommendations for the optimal energy for different conditions. The usual ranges are from 1 to 10J/cm² , but 16 to 24J/cm² have been suggested. In order to calculate the dosage, other parameters must be known, since each laser is different; these are the wavelength and power output : power density.

CAUTION

There is a risk of eye damage if the beam is applied directly to the eye. It can be reflected from any shiny surface, so remove, cover, or only switch on the laser beam when the applicator is in contact with the skin.

A laser should not be used for the direct treatment of neoplastic tissue.

Take care of your equipment.

Clean and sterilise the applicator before and after use.

CONCLUSION

Assessing whether a particular therapy is effective in promoting tissue healing is difficult, primarily because the old adage 'time heals all wounds' is largely true. Many diseases are self-limiting, and in these cases a horse's body is able to heal itself with no intervention whatsoever.

A fully functional, well rehabilitated horse is therefore the ultimate aim of most integrated therapies. This means restoring nerves, tendons and muscles to maximum capability, all leading to an injury-free animal, who is able to resume activity at a pre-injury level.

Practitioners and Their Approaches

There is now a huge awareness of the benefits of complementary therapies, both for humans and for horses. With his comparatively big, heavy body frame, the horse is particularly vulnerable to injury and damage as a result of falls and activity-associated accidents. Equally he may suffer considerable physical, and indeed mental trauma from bad riding, badly fitting tack, and inefficient stable management. The veterinary surgeon does not always have the answer to these problems, and this chapter investigates the increasingly important role of the osteopath, the massage therapist, the chiropractor, the physiotherapist, the acupuncturist and the healer in the horse owner's quest to restore and maintain the health and well-being of his horses.

Cranio-Sacral Therapy

CST is a gentle, hands-on method of evaluating and enhancing the function of the physiological body system called the 'cranial-sacral therapy system'; this system comprises the membranes and cerebrospinal fluid that surround and protect the brain and spinal cord. CST enhances the body's natural healing processes, and is effective for a wide range of medical problems associated with pain and dysfunction.

WHAT DOES IT TREAT?
The conditions that would be considered suitable for CST to treat include:

• traumatic brain and spinal cord injuries;
• stress- and tension-related problems;
• connective tissue disorders;
• colic;
• orthopaedic problems;
• central nervous system disorders;
• chronic neck and back pain;
• headaches;
• temporomandibular joint dysfunction (TMJ);
• birth-related difficulties.

The technique is increasingly used as a preventative health measure because of its ability to bolster resistance to disease and sustain overall good health.

Healthcare practitioners who might use CST in their work include veterinarians, chartered physiotherapists, osteopaths, chiropractors and healers.

HOW IS IT APPLIED?
A typical CST session lasts between 45 minutes and one hour. CST was developed by osteopath John E. Upledger, D.O., O.M.M., in the 1970s, and is based on theories of William Sutherland, D.O.

The horse can be treated sedated or non-sedated. The practitioner must have the permission of the horse owner's veterinary surgeon, and must complete a detailed written evaluation, including a full medical history and movement examination. The horse owner should be given full written aftercare instructions, and a follow-up appointment. It is important to ask what the horse will be allowed to do post treatment in terms of work and exercise, what should be done in terms of management, and if there is anything that ought not to be done.

The horse normally rests in a stable for the session, and the CST treatment involves the practitioner placing his hand over the cranium, sacrum or any other visceral or spinal point. There are no dramatic movements, but you should observe the horse gradually responding and his breathing rate changing.

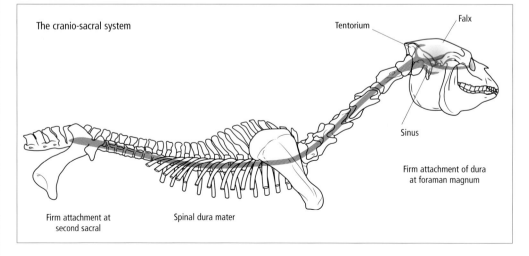

The cranio-sacral system

Tentorium

Falx

Sinus

Firm attachment of dura at foraman magnum

Firm attachment at second sacral

Spinal dura mater

Osteopathy

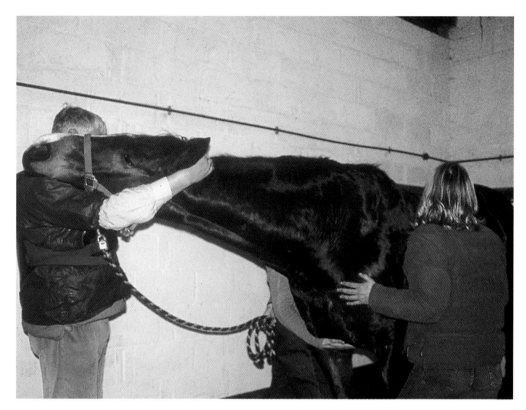

This is a system of healing discovered in the late nineteenth century by Dr A. T. Still in the USA. The principles of osteopathy are based on the applied knowledge of anatomy, physiology and pathology, namely that the body functions as an integral whole; that structure and function are inextricably bound up with each other; and that the body processes self-regulating mechanisms – meaning that it is able to cure itself.

HOW DOES IT WORK?
In practice this means that a problem has to be seen not only in its localised context, but also in the supposition that each posture structure may lead to pain (or other problems) in a remote part of the body (or that it may affect the entire body). The link between the two can be muscular, tendinous, fascial, neurological, visceral and/or arterial. Osteopaths treat according to these two basic principles, holistic

Osteopathic treatment includes the mobilisation of joints, see the full stretch of the horse's head and neck

and causal, and this often leads their attention to the spinal column, owing to its central role firstly as the axis of the body, but also as a housing of the nervous system. A detailed static and functional examination, plus the horse's history, should be recorded.

HOW IS IT APPLIED?
Osteopathic procedures can take place sedated, under general anaesthesia, or non-sedated. The treatment can be applied using different techniques, which may depend on the practitioner's experience and bias.

Some techniques are high velocity, small amplitude thrusts (manipulations); others are directed at mobilising the joints into the restricted range of motion. Sustained positional release incorporates a neurophysiological principle, and involves the reprogramming of movement and pain perception.

Aftercare may vary from a few days' rest, to several weeks, to months of rehabilitation. Generally the longer the problem has persisted, the more deeply the effects will have become engrained. Therefore the 'reprogramming' will require a longer time between sessions, and more applications of the treatment to secure a permanent effect.

Osteopathy under general anaesthetic to restore normal movement

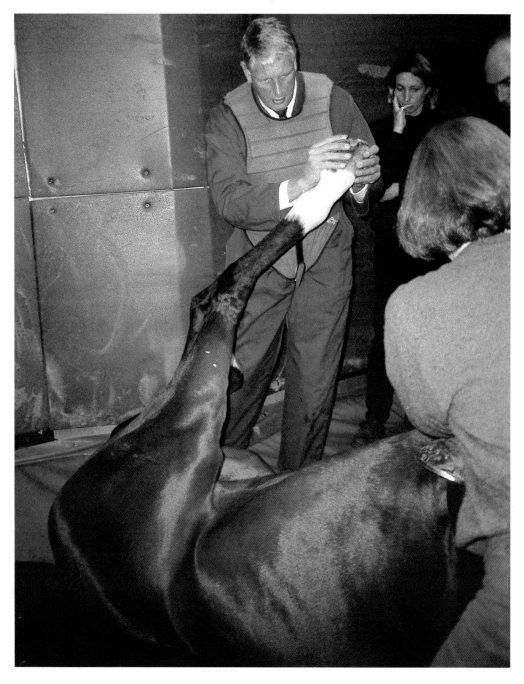

Equine Sports Massage

Professional sports massage techniques are applied to the horse, ostensibly for therapeutic purposes. It is argued that this will lead to increased performance levels and endurance, as well as helping to prevent injury. And in the event of injury, massage might increase circulation and reduce muscle tension and stress.

Most massage therapists are neither vets nor health-care professionals, and so there must be some caution attached to the lack of work-up and potential for diagnosis. Horses cannot talk, and therefore referred pain phenomenon, or secondary pain masquerading as stress points, or tissue that has lost its elasticity, can be wrongly attributed to

muscle that is not, in fact, a problem. A way round this potential pitfall of relying on the non-professional applying a therapy, is to ensure that it is used as a performance enhancer only, and that any injury or symptom is correctly identified by the veterinarian.

WHAT IS IT USED FOR?
Equine sports massage has several therapeutic uses; these include:

- to relax the horse before a competition;
- to alleviate stress after a competition;
- to help maintain well-being;
- to encourage and perpetuate the feel-good factor;
- to desensitise hypersensitive horses.

Massage can be taught to the owner or be performed by the physical therapist or masseur

The Bowen Technique

Thomas A. Bowen (1903–1982), who originated from Australia, developed the Bowen Technique, which allows the body to reset and heal itself. A Bowen treatment consists of a series of gentle moves on the skin or through the horse's rugs. The session normally lasts from half an hour to an hour, and can result in a deep sense of overall relaxation, allowing the body to recharge and balance itself. Delicate, light, gentle and precise touches, with frequent pauses, allow the body to respond and benefit.

It is used to benefit the immune and hormonal systems, and to help resolve musculoskeletal problems.

HOW DOES IT WORK?

Bowen encourages a gentle response that empowers the body's own responses to heal itself.

Note: Bowen does not purport to replace veterinary treatment, and it can only be used with veterinary consent.

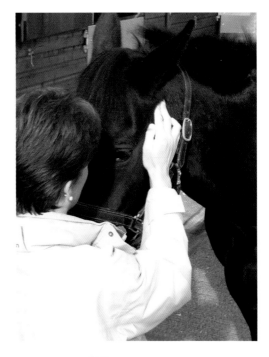

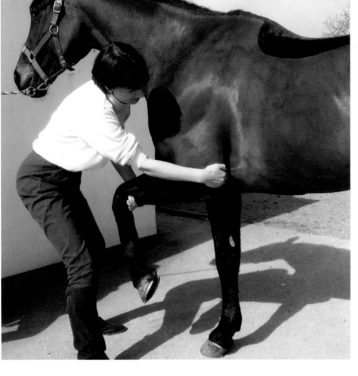

The Bowen Technique comprises of a series of small movements performed superficially to create a sensory effect, resulting in both local and general body changes

Chiropractic

Chiropractic is a profession that specialises in the diagnosis and treatment of conditions that are due to mechanical dysfunction of the joints and their effects on the nervous system. A vertebral subluxation is defined as a spinal misalignment or joint dysfunction, resulting in neurological or biomechanical dysfunction.

A 'chiropractic adjustment' is a short lever, high velocity, low amplitude (HVLA) controlled thrust, by hand or instrument, that is directed at specific articulations to correct vertebral subluxations and restricted movement of the pelvis and extremities. The adjustment produces an effect on the joint and surrounding muscles. It improves mobility, releases spasm and relieves pain.

Equine chiropractic care is not a substitute for traditional veterinary medicine or surgery: it offers a natural, drug-free adjunct to the horse's total health care. In conjunction with regular veterinary care, chiropractic treatment can decrease pain and add quality to the horse's performance, movement and well-being.

HOW DOES CHIROPRACTIC WORK?

Chiropractic patients generally have two major symptoms: pain and joint stiffness. The first is very difficult to measure; the second can be established more easily using range of movement (ROM) tests. It is usually very difficult to decide how much pain is due to the joint problem *per se*, or to the surrounding muscles being tight. The two symptoms are usually linked. Because of this, massage to 'loosen' tight muscles can provide

Chiropractic treatment allows normal spinal movement to be performed

As with any therapy always ensure your horse is sound in case the back problem is secondary to limb pain

temporary relief. However, the problem may recur if no treatment is administered to the problematic joint. In some circumstances, slow passive movement of the joints can induce more pain as the muscles tighten further; the chiropractic (HVLA) 'thrust', administered directly along the joint plane, must then be completed before the stretch is activated, thus avoiding further tightening of the muscles.

After chiropractic adjustment there is usually an immediate decrease in joint stiffness, which is measured as increased ROM, and there is also

REMEMBER: No chiropractic treatment should be administered without veterinary approval. The treatment will usually include:
• adjustments;
• soft tissue work (muscular trigger points);
• passive stretching;
• post treatment and preventative care advice.

A qualified chiropractor will be registered with the General Chiropractic Council, and chiropractors who treat animals will also have a specific 'Animal Chiropractic' qualification.

decreased muscle tension. It is difficult to measure decreased pain objectively, but a reduction of 'guarding' during movement would be expected: this is where the pain causes muscle tightness. Treatment resolves this, by the very rapid movement of joints (via the chiropractic adjustment) just beyond the normal physiological articular range.

WHAT IS IT USED FOR?
Certain signs and symptoms indicate that the horse is suffering from a problem or an injury that may benefit from chiropractic treatment; these include:

• display of pain or discomfort;
• uncharacteristic changes in behaviour or temperament;
• performance or movement problems;
• gait abnormalities;
• asymmetry (skeletal and muscular);
• muscle atrophy or spasm.

There are other circumstances besides these where chiropractic treatment may be appropriate; for instance, if the horse has difficulty chewing, and/or is unwilling to accept the bit, even after the teeth have been checked (a jaw or TMJ problem should be considered). Chiropractic treatment can also be used in maintenance care, as a general preventive measure.

Chiropractic treatment may not be appropriate if the animal has had recent trauma or surgery, or if any of the following are suspected:

• a bone-weakening pathology (i.e. cancer, osteoporosis);
• a fracture or dislocation (with signs of ligamentous rupture or instability);
• an infection;
• a vascular condition;
• malignant tumours.

Nor is it appropriate if there is profuse joint swelling, old surgical scars or skin lesions; or where the stress of being adjusted outweighs the possible benefits.

Equine Acupuncture

Acupuncture has been used for more than 3,000 years in China, but has only been widely practised in the UK since the 1970s.

WHAT IS IT USED FOR ?

Most of the acupuncture used in equine practice is either for the relief of chronic musculoskeletal pain, or to influence the function of internal organs. An example of the latter is the use of acupuncture to influence gut mobility in the treatment of colic. Acupuncture is particularly exciting because it has opened up a whole new range of treatment possibilities in general equine practice. Many patients that would previously have been left to wait and see what happened with the passage of time can now be actively treated. These include horses with chronic back pain and general malaise.

Only a qualified veterinary surgeon can perform acupuncture on animals. This is different from the situation in human medicine, where not all acupuncturists are doctors. IVAS is the qualification that is recognised worldwide.

WHAT IS ACUPUNCTURE ?

Acupuncture involves inserting fine, stainless steel needles through the skin at specific points on the skin called acupuncture points. This is known as 'dry needling'. Other types of acupuncture include:

- The injection of vitamin B12, local anaesthetic, homoeopathic medicines into acupuncture points with hypodermic needles.

Electroacupuncture being performed by a veterinary surgeon

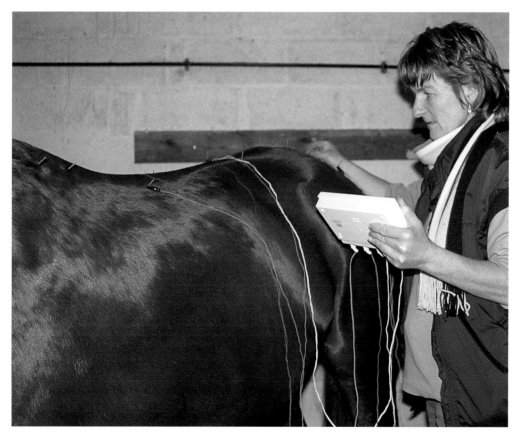

- Laser acupuncture, in which acupuncture points are stimulated by a laser. This has the advantage that there is no risk of infection, and the treatment is pain free.
- Electroacupuncture, which is the most often used for chronic pain. Needles are inserted into acupuncture points and stimulated electrically.
- Moxibustion, in which acupuncture points are heated by burning the herb *Artemisia vulgaris*, commonly called mugwort, on or above the skin. Commercially available 'moxa' sticks are available, where the burning end is moved slowly in a circular fashion over the point to be treated. It is especially useful for chronic muscular pain or arthritis.

Adverse Effects of Needling

The action of putting the needles into the skin carries with it a small risk of certain adverse effects such as the formation of haematomas; infection; 'stuck' needles; and needle breakage (though the risk in this instance is extremely small). These risks can be minimised by ensuring that the horse is suitably restrained, in a calm and relaxed state of mind, and that his coat is clean and dry. He is also best presented for treatment in a stable with a non-slip floor — rubber matting is ideal so that any dropped needles are easily retrieved.

KEYPOINT: Acupuncture should never be a traumatic experience either for the horse, the owner or the vet. Certain sedatives are thought to help the acupuncture take effect, and should be administered if the horse shows any signs of distress. Horses that have been in severe or chronic pain for some time should be sedated for the first, and possibly the second session.

Frequency of Treatment

Acute conditions are treated every one to three days, and longstanding problems once a week. When a horse has been chronically sore for many months, it is unrealistic to expect it to be 'cured' after one treatment. Most long-term conditions require four to five sessions to start with, and may need 'top-up' treatments once or twice a year. On the other hand, when acupuncture is used to treat colic, a single treatment is usually sufficient.

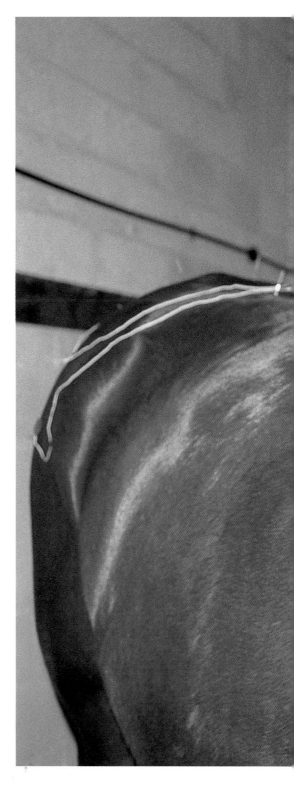

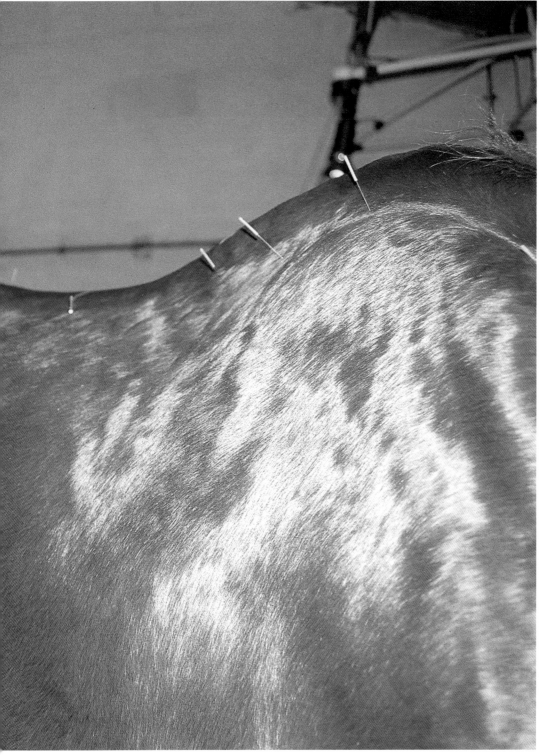

Acupuncture is usually tolerated well although some horses may need to be twitched or otherwise sedated

97

Response to Treatment

This is extremely variable, and it is important to recognise that there will be failures as well as successes. Following the first treatment, patients may be better, worse or the same. Most horses treated for musculoskeletal problems will show some degree of improvement after the first session. Very often the owners report that the horse seems much happier in itself. Subsequent treatments tend to give longer remissions, until the horse becomes pain free.

What is an Acupuncture Point ?

Acupuncture points are areas on the skin that overlie neurovascular bundles with many free nerve endings. They have a higher electrical conductivity when compared to the surrounding skin. They are commonly found over superficial nerve plexuses, at motor points close to where a nerve enters a muscle, at muscle-tendon junctions, on tendons and ligaments, and at locations where nerves emerge from within the skull.

SO HOW DOES ACUPUNCTURE WORK ?

By inserting the needles at carefully chosen points, an acupuncturist is able to influence and balance the flow of energy around the body. Acupuncture stimulates sensory nerve endings, and these transmit impulses to the brain. It then causes the transmission of information passing to and from the brain, and all other parts of the body.

These pathways have connections with the hypothalamus, and this accounts for the effect of acupuncture on regulatory mechanisms such as control of blood pressure, pulse, respiration, intestinal motility, hormone secretion, and white blood cell production. The hypothalamus is also responsible for emotions such as rage and aggression.

Conditions that would be suitable for treatment with acupuncture are:

• any painful condition;
• degenerative joint disease;
• muscle spasm (trigger point, myofascial syndrome);
• any imbalance of hormones or the immune system;
• respiratory conditions.

It can also be used to maintain the horse's general well-being. Note that it can be used safely alongside conventional medical treatment, and with other complementary therapies.

Physiotherapy

The first part of the training programme for a chartered animal physiotherapist or physical therapist is a human physiotherapy degree; only when they have completed this will they specialise in animal physiotherapy. Working on humans is an important part of the preparation for animal work, in that the student has the chance to develop observational and palpatory skills, aided and abetted by the patient's verbal responses.

A physiotherapy evaluation will incorporate a résumé of the horse's past and present-day history, plus a management assessment. A full account of any previous veterinary treatment should be given, and a direct line of communication between the veterinarian and physiotherapist maintained at all times. It is often very useful for them both to meet and to discuss the case together, and to share their short- and long-term aims.

WHAT IS IT USED FOR?
Physiotherapy is often used to assist in the following conditions:

- acute inflammation;
- chronic injury;
- pre- and post surgery;
- wounds;
- performance problems;
- general well-being;
- sports injuries;
- spinal (including neck) problems;
- nerve injuries;
- muscle damage;
- tendon and ligament injuries;
- secondary and compensatory problems;
- muscle atrophy.

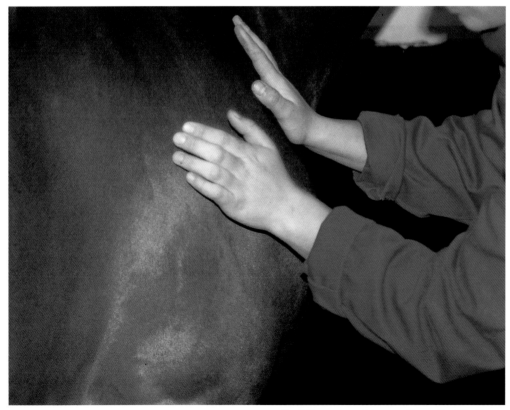

Physiotherapy is used to assess the quality of the tissues

Maintenance	Prevention	Treatment
Maximum flexibility	Maximum function	Assisting healing
Maximum strength Pain	Posture	Inflammation/ swelling
Enhanced performance	Identify risk factors	Electrotherapy and manual
	Therapies Monitor/ screening	Rehabilitation

- Restore movement using manipulation techniques to spine.
- Re-educate muscle control using muscle stimulation.

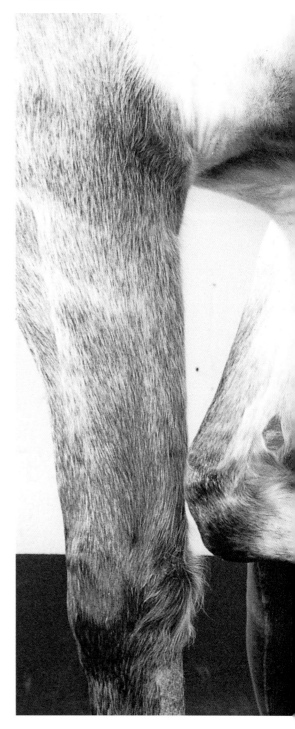

HOW DOES IT WORK?

A physiotherapist's most valuable tool is his hands, for palpating and locating areas of normal and abnormal function on the horse's body. Because of their understanding of anatomy, biomechanics, and veterinary and physiotherapy procedures, plus neurophysiology, physiotherapists can often detect subtle changes well before the onset of lameness or marked dysfunction.

The return-to-normal function will be assisted by the interplay between the appropriate use of treatments such as ice, ultrasound and also manipulative therapies. Getting the soft tissues working again, and restoring muscle tone, all help in maintaining correct joint alignment. The final stage is rehabilitating the horse so he can resume his normal, everyday job.

TYPICAL CASE SCENARIO

A steeplechaser who has fallen in his last race. History: mechanisms of injury and veterinary diagnosis.

- Gait evaluation.
- Palpatory and passive movement assessment.

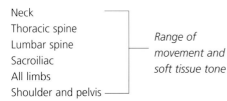

Neck
Thoracic spine
Lumbar spine
Sacroiliac
All limbs
Shoulder and pelvis

Range of movement and soft tissue tone

Methods

- Treat inflamed tissues with muscle stimulation and ultrasound.

- Teach exercises to maintain tissue and joint function.
- Use of schooling and poles to encourage full function.

Palpation, and assessment of the integrity of the tissues and joint structures allows the physiotherapist to identify abnormality

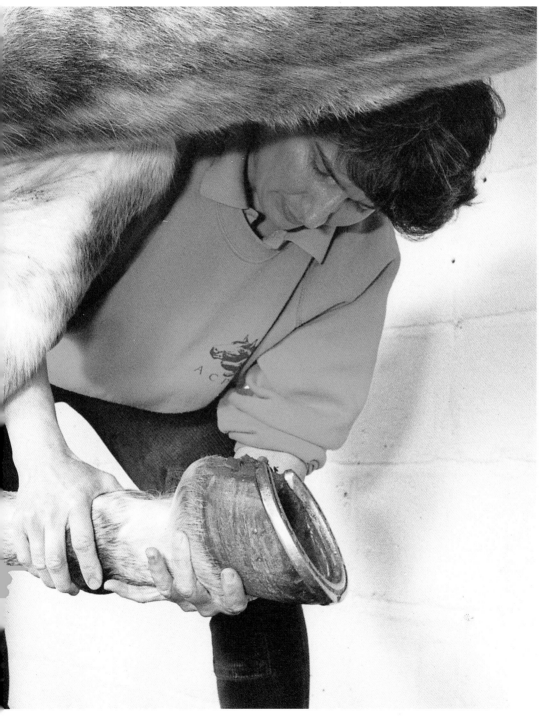

Healing

This is a useful therapy for integrating with conventional veterinary treatment for pain relief. It is also used in combination with other therapies because of its effects of relaxation and pain relief. The therapy of healing by using the hands as a channel for leading energy into the animal is an ancient form of medicine. Within every living being lies the life force or essence of the body – the spirit. It is a vibrant, oscillating field of energy, and healing aims to direct a positive flow to this life force and thereby release negative energy. The universe pulsates with energy, so each cell in a body vibrates and is in a constant state of dynamic change.

Where there is a problem in the body, lesions or blockages occur in the energy field, and the centres of energy within the body start to vibrate out of rhythm. It is not just the physical condition, but also the emotional state that affects this field.

The relaxed expression of the horse indicates clearly that he is enjoying the healing experience. Healing also helps the horse to release emotional blockage due to pain, box-rest and injury

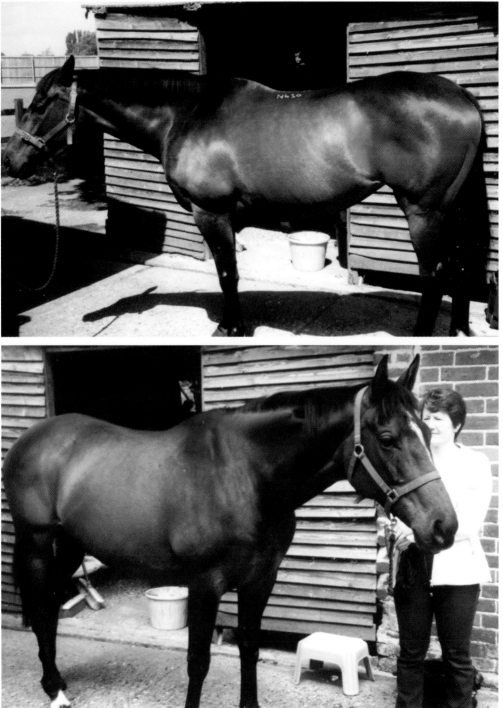

Before and after a healing session.
The horse, which at the time was being treated with the maximum dosage of bute, was quite clearly in pain.

Just 30 minutes later, the effects of an endorphin surge, brought about by the hands-on treatment, could be seen. The horse was much brighter and its outline had changed

HOW DOES IT WORK?

Healing involves laying the hands on to the horse's body to channel healing energy. It is done on a one-to-one basis, involving an exchange of energy between the healer, the one receiving it (e.g. the horse), and the creator (the spiritual source): it is gentle and non-invasive.

By strengthening the horse's body with healing, and by achieving physical stability, it is hoped that the horse will respond and begin to repair or stabilise from within. Healing can work emotionally, mentally or physically; imbalance in any of these areas in the horse can lead to illness, disease and behavioural problems. During a treatment, energy is transferred via the healer to the animal, and travels down lines of energy in the horse's body.

Healing can therefore be used as a preventative therapy, and also during illness and for maintenance.

Aftercare

- Once treatment has been carried out, ask what the rehabilitation plan is. You need to know what sort of time span you should be aiming at, such as when you can get on, when you can start schooling, when you can enter your next competition!
- Where the horse has been treated extensively, you cannot just pick up where you left off. You may have to work the horse in long reins or in-hand in order to develop the patterns of movement and neurophysiological function necessary to carry a rider.
- Some conditions will never be 'cured', but they may be helped, and will need continual 'topping up'.
- When asking for advice and subsequent treatment from a veterinarian or complementary practitioner, ask yourself if you want a quick cover-up, or a quality, superior result that costs more, takes longer to do, and will be harder sometimes to achieve?
- Always check with the vet and insurance company whether the complementary practitioner you are using is covered by your policy, and if they are qualified to do the job.

- If you are using more than one complementary practitioner, always make sure that they are aware of each other's approaches. Timing and planning are crucial to avoid overlap, or doubling up of effects in the treatment of your horse.
- Some treatments appear to have an immediate effect but do not withstand the rigours of life. These cases should be re-evaluated by the veterinarian, to confirm the diagnosis; however, it may be that a different type of complementary therapist or technique needs to be applied.

TO SEDATE OR NOT

Some practitioners prefer to sedate the horse once it has been seen moving, to enable an effective palpation and treatment session to be carried out. The reason for this is to allow the horse's brain to 'free wheel', and to suppress its flight instincts. The practitioner can still feel its pain and the decreased mobility of the tissues and structures, but now more effectively because of its more relaxed state. This is in part also to do with the enhanced pain relief that has been triggered by the use of pain-relief drugs with the sedation.

Managing the Horse at Home

Sensible management by owners and horse keepers is crucial to maintaining the horse in good health. Even if you do not need to use a vet, it is advisable to arrange for your horse to have a regular check-up by your vet, twice a year, to pre-screen for undiagnosed problems. The basic requirements of such a check-up should include:

- To walk, trot, and turn short on the hard and soft.
- To walk and trot on a 20m circle, on the hard.
- To walk, trot and canter on a soft surface.
- To check foot balance.
- To check teeth alignment and condition (a Hausmann gag should be used, so as to be able to check the back molars).
- To take a worm count, and/or blood test for normal levels.

The first three requirements test for lameness and/or back problems; the others are self-explanatory.

Comfortably fitting tack is just as important to the horse's well-being and performance, and qualified and respected professionals should check the saddle, harness and bridle twice a year.

This chapter also considers the best ways to care for the sick horse at home, and in particular how to cope with the horse that has to endure a spell of box-rest. Finally it investigates the properties and effects of certain medications that are available to the horse owner 'over the counter'.

Stable Management

REMEMBER:
- Your horse cannot talk.
- Trust your instincts.
- Use professionals.
- Don't bury your head in the sand.

Good stable management is essential in maintaining the horse in good physical shape, and keeping him happy. Thus the quality of the forage given, sensible use of supplements, and how you feed, will all contribute to his well-being. Moreover, behavioural problems are often the result of incorrect or insensitive stable management.

FORAGE

It is difficult to assess the quality of the forage you buy, because when you ask for a sample, it may not be representative of the whole delivery. Dusty, second-rate hay, in particular, will cause all sorts of wind-related problems because of the high spore numbers. However, it has been shown that there is a dramatic reduction in spore numbers when hay is soaked for half an hour. However, note that soaking for longer than this will reduce the nutrient value of the hay, requiring significant dietary supplementation if you do.

SUPPLEMENTS

When your horse is resting or is on good pasture, there is a tendency to reduce hard feed and hay

If you find that your horse spreads hay around the box and won't eat it, use a box or floor rack to contain it

intake. For the maintenance of health and repair, the body requires trace elements and minerals, so it is advisable to feed a good quality, broad-based supplement.

In certain cases specialist advice may be required to assess the effects of metabolic disease or immune-related conditions; you will also need advice if you live in an area with an imbalance of trace elements and minerals in the grass. In these cases work with your veterinary surgeon, who may also recommend a nutritionist.

FEEDING METHODS

The horse's jaw and teeth function best when he eats off the ground. This makes sense when you consider his digestive system evolved to cope with a constant supply of food for at least 16 hours a day as he roamed the plains eating grass and low-lying vegetation. Therefore in his stable environment, feed his hay and hard feed off the floor; this will aid his digestion, help his teeth alignment, assist the posture of his neck and back, and help to prevent respiratory problems (often caused by hay being fed in racks situated high up in the air).

Access to different forage in normal conditions is vital for the horse

107

Stable Vices

STEREOTYPIC BEHAVIOUR

Equine behavioural problems such as crib-biting, windsucking, weaving and box-walking, if repetitive and monotonous, are called stereotypic. If your horse has to be stabled for long periods on his own, or with a restricted outlook, it has been shown that using a mirror can reduce stress behaviour such as weaving, wood chewing and cribbing. Ensuring that there is an adequate outlook and plenty of opportunity to be close to other horses will also reduce stress. Diet, too, has been linked to the development of stereotypic behaviour: this is thought to be due to too little roughage and too high concentrate rations, which causes increased acidity in the gut.

Even foals may be susceptible to stereotypies: a recent study has indicated that the weaning

The weaning process should be as stress-free as possible to ensure the horse's long-term wellbeing

process itself induces this behaviour. The sudden separation and enforced isolation, plus the feeding of increased concentrate rations, have been shown to be causative factors. In one study, foals that received high concentrate rations early in life were at four times greater risk of developing crib-biting than those who did not. It has also been found that feeding silage or haylage increased the risk of stereotypic behaviour, especially wood-chewing; this is generally because a much smaller ration is fed, so the horse finishes it quickly and then has long periods with nothing to eat or to keep him occupied. With all this in mind, the following recommendations might be considered:

- Foals are not box-weaned.
- Horses are turned out as much as possible.
- If hay replacers or concentrates are fed, do this very slowly and in combination with an ad lib supply of grass or hay.

Stereotypic behaviour, such as crib-biting, can be induced by stress

Health Check List

It is as well to know your horse's normal parameters, so that you are immediately alert to any change in his appearance or behaviour.

BREATHING

When normal, breathing is hardly noticeable. Watch the flanks – the horse should breathe about eight to twelve times a minute. Any increase in this rate in the resting horse is abnormal, especially when accompanied by 'heave lines'. This may be noticed in horses with chronic pulmonary disease.

Any discharge, both first thing and after exercise, should be noted and discussed with your veterinary surgeon. A foul-smelling discharge may be evidence of an infected sinus.

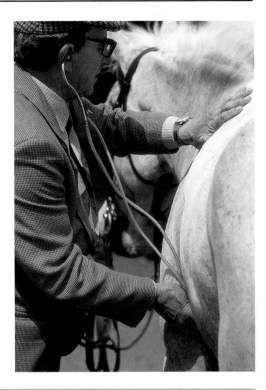

Right: Regular monitoring of the heart rate will aid early detection of possible problems

Below: This horse clearly demonstrates a 'heave' line

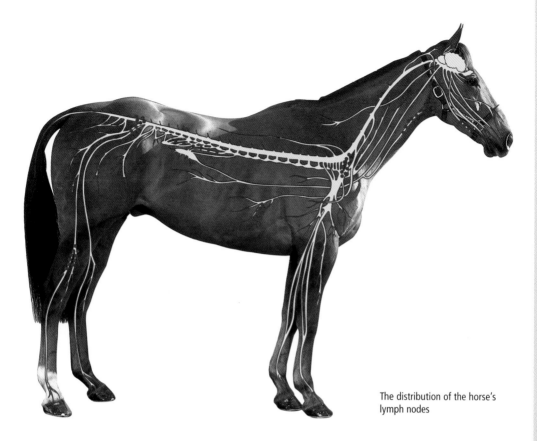

The distribution of the horse's lymph nodes

HEART AND CIRCULATION

The normal heart rate is between thirty-five and forty-five beats per minute; it can best be heard behind the point of the left elbow. An increase will be caused by exercise, stress or pain.

BLOOD TESTS

These are used to test for the horse's health status, and to identify possible reasons for poor performance, or ill health. Different blood proteins are analysed to see whether there is any liver, muscle or worm damage.

Muscle enzyme levels can be measured: if the muscle wall becomes damaged, muscle enzyme levels rise. Their detection is therefore useful to diagnose and monitor muscle damage. A significant rise – for example 3,000 to 30,000

— indicates azoturia or 'tying up'. A smaller or temporary rise will occur with any muscle damage, such as a muscle spasm or strain. Regular monitoring is therefore necessary to assess recovery.

For competition horses it is a good idea to have periodic 'normal' blood samples taken, as a yardstick.

OTHER PARAMETERS

• Infection: makes the horse dull; he will be off his food.
• Temperature: a horse's normal temperature is 37–38°C. This will be raised if he has an infection.
• Lymph nodes: these can sometimes be swollen and painful. In the head these can be found under the jaw.

111

Caring for the Box-Resting Horse

Nursing a sick horse can be demanding and time-consuming. The added burden of watching an animal become visibly stressed by its confinement can make the task of nursing all the more difficult. In order to help horses deal with confinement while on box-rest, particularly those individuals who are perky enough to want to be out, a plan of action can be drawn up that follows just a few simple rules dictated by the horse's natural behaviour and environment.

Horses at grass will graze for long periods of time with short rest periods in between

FEEDING BEHAVIOUR

The horse's digestive anatomy and physiology suits the trickle feeder (little and often). In its natural environment the horse grazes, from a seasonally varying menu, for about 16 out of the 24 hours in the day, selecting from a variety of available plants. The horse is a social animal that would normally graze when other members of the herd were grazing. Obviously for some sick horses, particularly after surgery, there are specific feeding regimes that need to be followed. However, for most horses that have been laid off work, there are a few simple rules to follow.

First of all, a horse on box-rest requires less energy than that of the same individual in work, and it should therefore be offered a low energy, high forage diet (unless otherwise indicated by the veterinarian). If the volume of concentrates is reduced below the minimum recommended amount, remember to add a good quality vitamin/mineral supplement to make up the shortfall – speak to the nutritionist or helpline of the concentrate manufacturer. Horses seek variety in their diet, and particularly those stabled for long periods can become very tired of the same feed. This can be managed simply by offering them a selection of different types of forage at any one time so as to mimic their natural environment.

Ideally horses should be feeding for long continuous periods, so forage should not be restricted (offer ad lib hay); alternatively you could try extending the feeding period by using small-mesh haynets occasionally (although any

A horse on box rest needs to be well managed to allow it to be happy and stress free

advantage in this has to be measured against the disadvantages to posture and teeth alignment), and by presenting concentrates or high fibre pellets in something like a 'feedball': the horse has to push this around the floor in order for the food inside to drop out of the small holes punched in it.

If a boxed horse is reluctant to feed, often the sight of another horse eating will be enough to reassure it, and encourage it to do likewise. When regaining appetite after illness, stimulate the senses by offering small, palatable meals. Do not leave uneaten feed in the bowl or manger for long periods, but take it away and re-offer after an interval. Finally, the benefits of grazing the horse in hand should never be underestimated, and this should be done if allowed.

COPING WITH RESTRICTED MOVEMENT

The modern horse evolved essentially as a plains dweller, ranging up to 80km per day, exploring and roaming over wide open spaces. The horse is, therefore, strongly motivated to keep moving, not necessarily at high speeds, but certainly over some distance.

In the wild, horses would not voluntarily put themselves in a small, confined area from which they can neither effectively scan their environment nor escape, both their flight response and the opportunity to explore curtailed. And while it is necessary to keep some horses on box-rest, they will lose the strength in their muscles and have reduced circulation, in exactly the same way as a person confined to bed. So if the horse's condition allows, and in conjunction with the vet and a chartered physiotherapist, a programme of exercise consisting of massaging and suppling exercises can be performed.

It may be possible to use a small turnout area, such as a round pen or small fenced off area, as a progression from complete box-rest to turnout.

With the horse at home, the owners should be encouraged, if appropriate, to spend the time they would have spent riding or training the horse, in handling it, grooming it, and giving it remedial exercise. Both the horse and owner will benefit from the physical contact and the time spent together, and by making sure that at least parts of the body will not remain unused, the recovery back to full work should therefore be more successful.

The following therapies can all be practised in the box:

- bodywork – Shiatsu;
- healing – relieves stress, and pain relief;
- the 'Tellington' Equine Awareness method;
- physiotherapy.

Opposite: Box-rest is sometimes essential to allow the union of a fracture. Movement or weight bearing at the critical stage could result in permanent disability and it may be necessary to put the horse in a sling

Right: Shiatsu is used to complement other therapies and to assist healing

SENSORY STIMULATION

The horse evolved in an environment where it was a prey species; therefore in order to survive, it is motivated to constantly appraise its environment. Although we may assume the stable to be a safe, warm place, for a horse it may represent a restriction of these survival techniques. For some horses on box-rest, a quiet, undisturbed corner in the yard is the best place, and the condition of the horse and its normal temperament will have a bearing on that decision. However, many horses will benefit from some sensory stimulation, though over-excitement should be avoided. Offer these animals a changing environment by stabling them in a box from which they can see the activities of the yard. If there are back or side windows in the box, open them up (if the period of box-rest is going to be a long one, then having alternative views is crucial). If you can lead the horse out without risk to his rehabilitation, then do so, and take him to a different spot each day — it need only be a small distance — to explore a different part of the yard.

Left: Hand grooming by the carer can give sensory stimulation and aid relaxation and pain relief

Below: The use of stable 'toys' may help to prevent boredom which may manifest itself in stereotypic behaviour

KEY POINTS:
- A box-rested horse should receive a low energy concentrate and high forage diet: in short, a fibre-based diet, including ad lib hay (unless otherwise stated by the veterinarian).
- Spend time grooming, massaging and suppling (as indicated by the condition of the horse).
- Extend feeding duration with small-mesh haynets and feeding devices such as a 'feedball'.
- Offer visual stimulation such as interesting scenery or visitors, and olfactory stimulation such as herbs and other horses.
- Mental stimulation such as stable toys should be provided at random intervals.
- Ensure a friendly horse is in the next box, or visits frequently, so that they can spend time communicating with each other.

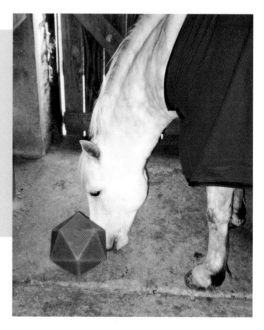

Mental stimulation is also required, and stable toys should be used to keep the horse alert and interested. Box-rest may compromise a horse's respiratory function (confined air space, hay and bedding spores, and an unnatural head position if the horse spends the entire period looking over the door). So time spent with his head down, a natural position that encourages drainage of the respiratory tract, is vital: he should therefore be encouraged to feed, explore and play with his neck stretched down towards the ground. Hide carrots or treats in appropriate places around his place of confinement so he has to puzzle out where they are, or how to get them.

Stable toys can be hung up, or played with on the ground -- you should use a combination of both, preferably hanging them against the wall to prevent them swinging around too much in the air. We are advised not to leave toys in the box the whole time: evidently research has shown that the stimulus to play and explore is diminished if the object is always there, so introduce the different toys at random, and from time to time leave the horse without anything in his box at all — his interest will be renewed when his toys reappear.

SOCIAL BONDS

In the natural environment no horse lives in isolation: every horse will live within a group. Thus a basic need is horse companionship, or at the very least a human friend who will touch and groom him – and he needs to allow himself to be groomed back. Research indicates that the use of mirrors helps to reduce confinement stress by allowing him to see an image of himself, which moves. (Mirrors should be made of non-breakable glass or Perspex.)

In short, once the horse has been made as comfortable as his condition allows, the owner's main tasks are to maintain gut function, keep his mind and body stimulated through all his senses, and offer him companionship.

The use of mirrors in the stable has been shown to prevent weaving

Medication for the Injured Horse

In the past, poultices, liniments, bandaging and hosing were the only 'hands-on' options for soothing soft tissue soreness and joint pains. Then 'bute' — phenylbutazone — became the drug of choice for general old-age lameness and stiffness, as well as inflammation in specific body parts. However, bute is banned for use in competition horses, and it is not seen by owners to be very proactive in the prevention of structural changes, or for reversing their progress.

So people then started to look for products that worked not just to abate the pain to make the horse feel better, but to heal and work maximally, perhaps actually to improve the quality of joints and soft tissue. Some of these products are injectable drugs for the treatment of joint conditions, others are unregulated oral or topical supplements. The former are for the vet to administer; the latter are supported by anecdotal evidence, giving credence to their effects, and more recently by scientific evidence, albeit sparse. Their intention is to:

• reduce toxic by-products of injury and inflammation;
• physically improve joint and muscle-fibre lubrication;
• boost the production of healthy tissue;
• re-establish normal immune activity.

> **KEY POINT:** Medicating athletic horses for the sole purpose of eliminating their pain is rarely a wise idea. However, caught early enough, treatment may prevent a more advanced stage of the disease process.

MANAGING INFLAMMATION

The chemicals associated with inflammation are known as fatty acids, or free radicals, and the hormone that is involved is prostaglandin. In concentration these do harm, prolonging and enlarging the inflammatory reaction beyond the level needed to tidy up the original injury. Bute and/or NSAIDs intercept the chemical 'cascade' that triggers and maintains inflammation; they block prostaglandin activity, and others, and reduce both the inflammatory reaction and also the perception of pain.

On the down side, however, the long-term administration of NSAIDs can lead to irritation and ulceration of the intestine.

ANTIOXIDANTS

These are certain vitamins, minerals and enzymes that clear out the toxic free radicals at the site of tissue trauma, and thereby assist in reducing inflammation. The end result is to facilitate healing.

Example 1: Vitamin E works with the mineral selenium; a deficiency can cause 'wobbler syndrome' and episodes of 'tying up'. It is suggested that this combination enhances the health of joint cartilage. Vitamin E is also a player in immune function and reproductive health.

Note that too much selenium can cause problems, therefore check the level before adding it.

Example 2: MSM (methyl sulfonyl methane) is a dietary derivate of DMSO, with anti-inflammatory properties. It can apparently also help improve lung function, reduce allergic responses, enhance circulation, and help horses to cope with stress. It has been studied more in humans, and suggests a high safety margin.

LUBRICANTS

These are substances and drugs with specific benefit to cartilage, and include unregulated oral supplements. They are generally given orally, or they are injected with specific animal-derived proteins identical to their own cartilage and joint fluid components. These proteins migrate to the joints via the bloodstream, or are injected there directly (this would be strictly the remit of your veterinarian). The consequent reduction in inflammation and destructive enzymes in the joints, plus the presence of healthy lubricants, encourages the cartilage to produce more normal synovial fluid. This effectively stops the destructive spiral, even if it does not actually heal existing

Horses can be encouraged to take their medicines by offering it from the hand

cartilage damage. Manufacturers of such dietary compounds say that the same thing occurs when horses eat these animal-derived proteins, and there are some scientific studies to back the claims.

NUTRACEUTICALS

A nutraceutical is any non-toxic food component that has demonstrated health benefits. They are substances that can be administered orally to provide agents required for normal body structure and function, and are given with the intent of improving the health and well-being of the animal. Some are vitamins and minerals that are normally included in the diet at some minor level, but when fed at a higher dosage are reputed to carry some specific benefit; for example, the B-vitamin biotin, said to improve the quality of the hoof horn.

Some are herbal in composition, such as Echinacea, garlic and valerian, and are assumed to have helpful effects, based on their use in humans. Others are basically chemical, designed to replace compounds that the horse might be lacking in his own body – for instance chondroitin sulphate, a component of healthy cartilage, is one.

KEY POINT: Most have not received scientific scrutiny as the expense is too high, and it is not in the companies' interest to do so.

Rehabilitation

Once a horse has recovered from physical trauma and completed all necessary treatment, he will almost certainly need to build up his strength and muscle tone before he is able to resume a training programme or any sort of fitness regime. This period of rehabilitation may take some time, depending on the severity of his injury and the length of time he was laid off, and he will benefit from activities in which he does not have to carry the weight of a rider. Lungeing is always helpful, and certain training aids, correctly applied, will certainly help in building up his physique: the Pessoa training system, taping, and the Tellington-Jones Equine Awareness method and TTouch, are all considered, amongst others, in this chapter.

Lungeing

There are certain ways of doing things when you are lungeing your horse, and other things that you shouldn't do: so check the list below before you set out with your recuperating horse.

You should always:

- Select the surface carefully – too loose, and weak limbs will have to work too hard, at risk of possible injury. Start on a firmer surface (though avoiding a concussive effect), and progress to a less stable one to increase the physical demands.
- Use appropriate tack for the horse's stage of recovery, and to encourage correct movement.
- Warm the horse up before commencing intensive work on the lunge.
- Vary the size of the circle, depending on the fitness and athletic ability of the horse, namely, larger for the less mobile and those at an earlier stage of rehabilitation. In very weak or problematic cases use a rectangle, and use the whole of the school for your circles.
- Vary the pace on the lunge by lengthening and shortening the strides in each gait.
- Make frequent transitions.
- Maintain a light contact when the horse is doing what you ask, to avoid head-tilting.
- Sometimes include a small jump or trotting poles (but do not use side reins).
- Observe if he is tracking up correctly (are his hind feet landing in the same place as his fore limbs?). When asking for lengthened strides, the hind feet should overstep more.
- Observe the activity of his back, and his fore- and hindquarter muscles. Look for a relaxed, loose movement.
- If his mouth and/or neck are a problem, then attach the lunge line to the side of the nose. This exerts a better directional pull on the head, and should avoid any head-tilting.
- Observe the position of the limbs as they move. They should not interfere with each other, causing injury. Wear brushing boots to protect against this, and to monitor its occurrence (marks will be left on the boot from brushing).
- Don't lunge a horse for too long when he is

weak, or physically immature. It can be physically exhausting, so take great care.
- Don't let him become bored.
- Don't let the horse go too fast. This can cause damage, and does not teach him impulsion.
- Don't lunge in too small an area. A few small circles are good gymnastically, at the appropriate

time in his rehabilitation. But the circle should always be large enough to allow him to canter forwards comfortably.

LUNGEING IN A RECOVERY PROGRAMME
- Vary the horse's gait and speed on the lunge, and use frequent transitions.
- Use trotting poles, two or three on a circle to start with, flat on the ground, then progress to raising one end, then both ends.
- Position a telegraph pole at each corner of the school, and lunge over these.
- Lunge up and down slopes of varying gradient and at different speeds and gait (do not use side reins). Let him do this slowly to start with.
- Use the diameter of the circle to increase the demands of the exercises: the smaller the circle, the harder it will be for the horse.

The use of carefully placed poles will facilitate the development of mobility

Training Aids

Before using any training aid, check that you know how to fit it, and ask a qualified instructor to teach you how to use it. Ensure that your horse is at a suitable stage of his rehabilitation programme to be working in the way the training aid positions him, and check that there is no physical reason preventing him from doing what you want, such as pain in his teeth, or poll, or back.

THE 'PESSOA' TRAINING SYSTEM

This training system is designed to work the horse in four different positions, encouraging balance and a gradual building up of muscle along the horse's topline. On the lunge, the horse should be encouraged to engage the quarters, as the system works on the principle of pulleys and levers. If the horse resists by lifting the head and nose, there is pressure on the bars of the mouth, and the hindquarters; when he drops his head or gives with his jaw, the pressure is removed.

Note that some horses need time to become used to the breeching, so introduce it slowly.

The Pessoa Training Aid

THE 'CHAMBON' TRAINING SYSTEM

The Chambon system is designed to be used on the lunge, or for loose-schooling sessions. It helps to establish steady, rhythmic trotwork, and encourages the horse to work in a longer, lower profile. It helps to engage the hindquarters and build up the muscles of the topline. It encourages the horse to lower his head, but does not ask for flexion at the poll. The horse learns to drop his head and carry the head and neck low and extended, but he is still able to poke his nose.

The Chambon is particularly useful for a horse with a weak back or with muscles that have built up incorrectly on the underside of the neck. However, it works the hindquarters very thoroughly, so care must be taken not to work the horse too long, as he will become tired quickly. Adjust it gradually, so that it will only be felt if he lifts his head too high, with a hollow back.

With care, and regular, short sessions, he will be encouraged to lower his profile. The topline muscles are then strengthened and built up so that the horse eventually finds it natural and comfortable to adopt a lower, more relaxed way of going.

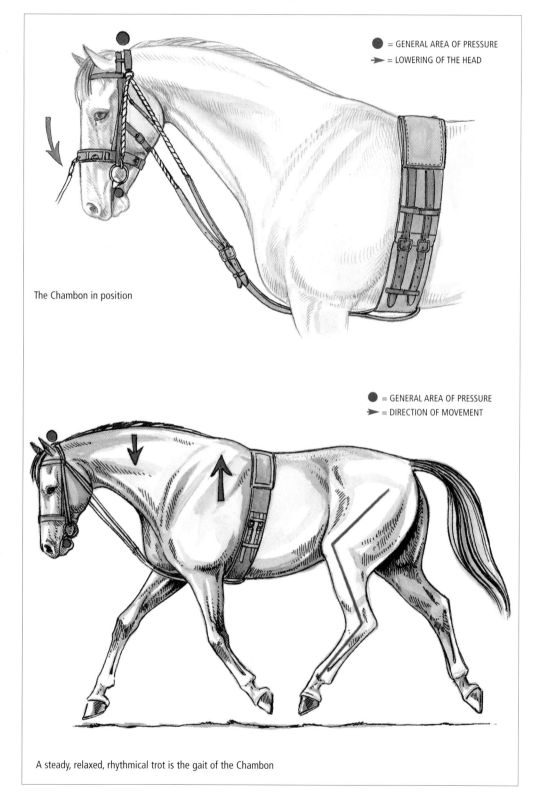

= GENERAL AREA OF PRESSURE

= LOWERING OF THE HEAD

The Chambon in position

= GENERAL AREA OF PRESSURE

= DIRECTION OF MOVEMENT

A steady, relaxed, rhythmical trot is the gait of the Chambon

TTEAM

The Tellington-Jones Equine Awareness Method and TTouch was developed by Linda Tellington-Jones, an experienced horsewoman, for training horses; it represents a combining of her training of the Feldenkrais teachings, and her experience of massage and physical therapy.

TTEAM ground exercises in effect influence behavioural and physical problems by dramatically expanding and improving a horse's capacity for learning and co-operation, and by improving both his balance and his co-ordination.

The Tellington TTouch is a series of circular touches of the hands and fingers intended to activate cellular function and to further deeper communication and understanding between horse and trainer. For each TTouch, hands and fingers are held in different positions and applied with varying pressure, depending on the effect desired.

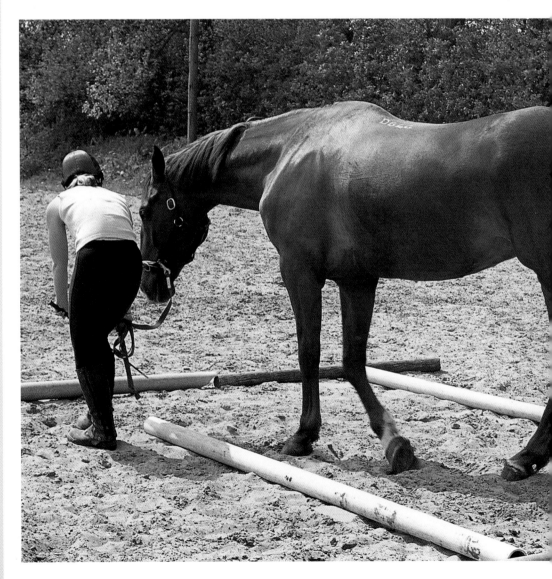

The bodywrap can be worn in the stable, for in-hand work and when ridden. It provides sensory information on body position and muscle activity

The TTouch is used to encourage and increase relaxation, improve athletic ability, introduce a new sense of awareness, enhance healing, and reduce stress in performance horses.

The ground exercises are specifically designed to guide the horse into non-habitual movements, which increase the ability to learn. The obstacles are another integral aspect of the TTEAM ground exercises: they teach both horse and handler to use his or her body in a way that improves balance, self-control, precision, fine motor skills and eye/hoof co-ordination.

Horses with major neurological weaknesses through to young horses developing strength will benefit from working through the TTEAM labyrinth

Taping

Taping to reduce musculoskeletal pain and improve movement patterns has been used in human treatment and rehabilitation. Chartered physiotherapist Narelle Stubbs has pioneered this approach for use in horses.

Taping can be used to reduce movement-associated pain. Based on a thorough assessment of presenting movement patterns and pain mechanisms, it can be used as a useful treatment approach in itself, or as a means of maintaining treatment effects. The effect can last for hours, even days, supplementing the relatively brief therapist-patient contact.

Taping can be used to affect pain directly by offloading irritable trigger points and fascial pain. It appears to be effective at proprioceptive, mechanical and pain-relieving levels.

> **KEY POINT:** We normally use tape for only short periods because there is no suitable tape for prolonged use.

Example 1: Tape is applied in such a way that there is little or no tension while the limb is held or moved in the desired direction. But when the tissues are taken beyond this point the tape will be under tension, creating a sensory effect that will be perceived by the brain. Over time this will result in a new movement pattern that does not go out of the desired range.

Example 2: If tape is used on muscles that are underactive, by taping in the shortened position, increased force can be generated at the beginning of the movement.

General Rules for Successful Taping
- A thorough assessment is required to identify the horse's habitual resting posture, and for movement faults.
- The skin must be prepared: it needs to be clean and dry.
- The body parts must be well positioned.
- Use hypoallergenic tape without tension, and then tape with tension (duct tape).
- The taping is continued until the horse has learned to actively control movement in the desired way; or the effects on symptoms are maintained when it is not worn.
- Taping should not be used if there is any adverse reaction from the skin, or if the horse is at all nervous of the procedure.

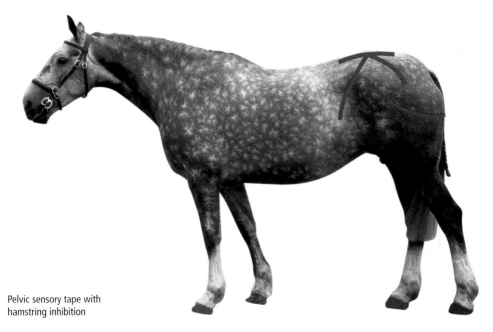

Pelvic sensory tape with
hamstring inhibition

Case Studies

Every horse should be treated as an individual. There are no recipe books for treatment, only guidelines and thought processes which allow professionals and owners to make sound clinical judgements based on past and present knowledge. People often fall into the trap of listening to too much 'good advice' or by not following a plan of action through to its completion. Communication is vital and re-evaluation critical. Never attempt to pre-diagnose a condition, it's never that simple! Horses continue to astound me by their remarkable ability to be masters of disguise and others to all apart at the seams easily, whilst others can go on forever. They are, perhaps, far more complex than we ever really give them credit for.

Colic and Gait Irregularity

CASE STUDIES

'Jack' is a 12.3hh, 17-year-old Irish pony; he came from a riding school, and had just been purchased, with no vetting. The history of his condition may be summarised thus:

- Loss of appetite after two weeks
- Increasing hind limb stiffness
- Bouts of colic
- Loss of condition
- He was seen by the veterinary surgeon, the horse dentist and the nutritionalist

VETERINARY EVALUATION

He reacted badly to antispasmodic drugs, so was unable to receive further medication for colic. Also, blood tests revealed that he had a virus, and that he had probably had it for some time.

DENTIST

His teeth were checked, and although some work was required, they were not in a bad enough state to prevent loss of appetite.

NUTRITIONALIST

He was given 'Be Sure' to stimulate his appetite, and the mineral and trace element supplement 'Sure Limb' to provide his baseline needs and nutritional support.

COMPLEMENTARY THERAPIES

Veterinary acupuncture: Acupuncture was used to assess for painful trigger points and the abnormal gait of the hind limbs. Trigger points were found between the hamstrings. His abnormal hindlimb gait was attributed to a fibrotic myopathy.

The bladder and digestion meridians were stimulated for appetite, and the trigger points of the hamstrings were also needled.

Healing: Due to the change of environment after ten years, and because of the ongoing effects of the virus, 'Jack' had very low energy levels. Healing was used to help with pain relief and the stimulation of general well-being.

OWNER MANAGEMENT

It was important for Jack's digestion that he was fed little and often; he was also given various types of hay to keep him interested in food, and this was soaked for thirty minutes before it was fed.

Initially due to the virus, 'Jack' was not exercised for three weeks. Blood testing was used to assess his condition, and to evaluate his health status.

KEY POINT: Soaking hay for 30 minutes reduces spores. Soaking for longer causes no further reduction in spores, but the nutrient value of the forage is affected.

TACK

Jack's bridle seemed a shade too small, so the browband was changed for a bigger one that wasn't too tight across the front of his head. The saddle was also closely inspected to ensure that

KEY POINT: A riser pad prevents the rider's weight being placed unevenly and too far back on the horse's back

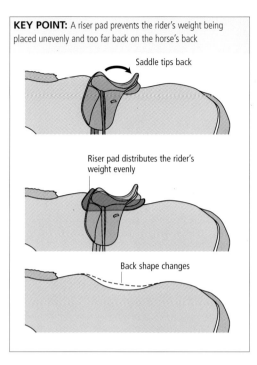

Saddle tips back

Riser pad distributes the rider's weight evenly

Back shape changes

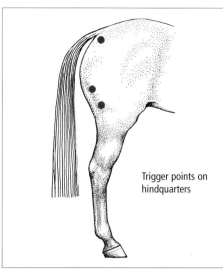

Trigger points on hindquarters

there was no internal asymmetry, and that it sat correctly on the pony, as he had lost muscle and body condition. For a couple of weeks he wore a riser pad under the saddle to help balance it, though after this time his topline had improved so substantially that it was removed.

TIP: On reflocking, or if your horse dislikes being saddled or ridden, ask the saddler to check the following points on the saddle: the symmetry of the girth straps on to the tree, the position of the stirrup bars, and their potential for bruising. He should also assess the general condition of the saddle, and also its potential to aggravate the conformation of the horse.

PHYSIOTHERAPY PERFORMED BY THE OWNER
Trigger points:
• Compression therapy applied to improve circulation and release spasm

Mobilisation exercises
• Hock flexion
• Upper limb circles
  (Ref: *The Injury Free Horse*, Sutton 2001)

Stretching
• Hamstring stretches x 2, for 15sec
  (Ref: *The Injury Free Horse*, Sutton, 2001)

Basic massage techniques can be used to assist long-term management

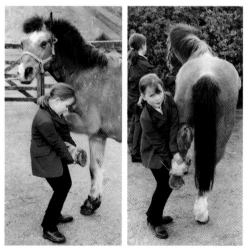

Owners can be taught safe exercises to help maintain suppleness

Performance Problem

This case dealt with an eight-year-old advanced event mare; she had an eighteen-month history of sporadic performance problems, particularly in the showjumping phase.

SIGNS/SYMPTOMS

On close inspection, the mare showed the following irregularities:

- excessive wear of the left hind foot;
- abnormal muscle development of the hindquarters;
- underside of the neck over-muscled from poor posture;
- palpable soft tissue swelling of the midline lumbar sacral area;
- trick movements of the cervical spine on testing;
- poor stability of the hocks and pelvis on testing;
- change of gait pattern – she was moving much more closely behind, with high knee action, and decreased flexibility on one rein.

VETERINARY EVALUATION

Both flexion tests and nerve blocks were positive for the front feet, and radiography presented minimal changes in the navicular bones.

The diagnosis was navicular syndrome; it was decided that the farrier and the vet would resolve the foot pain.

Re-evaluation after several months concluded that the patient was still not sound and not coping with the work. After further veterinary evaluation, gamma scintigraphy was performed, with the following diagnosis:

- there was a high suspensory inflammation of the left hind limb;
- bi-lateral sacroiliac strain;
- lower cervical 'hot-spots' (the X-rays showed changes, but they were not considered significant);
- and the navicular bones were very hot.

It was decided that the management plan would include physiotherapy and good farriery before yet another veterinary re-evaluation.

PHYSIOTHERAPY

The most likely cause of the damage to the skeleton that was revealed on the gamma scintigraphy was a fall. This, combined with the secondary effects from adapting to the foot pain, had led to an abnormal posture and mechanics of movement.

Observation, palpation and movement testing revealed an abnormal muscle tone, and decreased range of motion of the joints and associated soft tissues. Treatment was used to correct the information received by the brain from the body, and the correct responses to the organs and muscles initiated.

Manual therapy was used to release muscle spasm and to decrease pain, and to effect these changes.

RE-EVALUATE THE PROBLEM

A complex problem such as this case takes time to resolve. Continual re-evaluation, even after return to full work, is essential to 'nip in the bud' any adaptation to the problems identified, or the development any new ones.

REHABILITATION

The aims of this phase of the mare's recovery were to teach normal movement, and to improve strength and flexibility; this would be done in three stages:

Stage 1:
- Proprioceptive body taping
- Use of 'chains' for sensory limb placement
- Long-reining and body ropes
- Slow fittening exercise

CHAINS: Chains are placed around the fetlock and consist of different weights. They aid the horse's awareness of that particular limb, but are used for short periods of time only.

Stage 2:
- Use of endurance and strength training
- Up and down hills
- Across hills
- Poles
- Pessoa training aid

Stage 3:
- Bounce fences
- Grids
- Fast work

Back to competition – total time, nine months.

Long-reining can form part of the Stage 1 of the rehabilitation programme

Degenerative Joint Disease

'Ben' is a 13.2hh, 17-year-old Pony Club pony. He was on loan to an eight-year-old girl. In his previous home he was ridden by a fourteen-year-old boy. He was re-homed, as it was felt he had been outgrown. He had a history of refusing when show jumping at jumps over 2ft 6in.

SIGNS/SYMPTOMS

Initially he performed well at the lower levels (up to 2ft 3in). However, his back seemed to have changed shape, and his saddle was tilting back too much, so the new owners called the saddler. The saddler compromised by fitting a riser pad to correct this, but commented on the asymmetric muscling through the back and over the withers. I was asked to give an opinion on the reason for this.

ASSESSMENT FINDINGS

Passive movement testing identified decreased range of motion of the left hind into extension and full flexion. The right forelimb also did not like to be pulled forwards into extension. His muscles were generally sore, and he had an inverted posture – that is, he held his head high and dipped his back. I observed him being exercised on the soft and on the hard, and on the lunge on the hard he was lame on both reins on the inside forelimb. On examination he had poor forelimb conformation, and due to his age and history I predicted he had lower limb pain.

VETERINARY DIAGNOSIS

The vet performed nerve blocks and then foot x-rays. There was evidence of general degenerative changes, especially around the navicular bone.

TREATMENT

This consisted of eggbar shoes and cortaflex. A course of massage and deep soft-tissue work plus chiropractic was given to manage the soft tissue and joint dysfunction.

OUTCOME

Ben has returned to the Pony Club with the knowledge of his underlying condition which has resulted in more maintenance measures and management issues being actioned.

Osteoarthritis of the Stifle

Aged New Forest gelding, not ridden but retired to the field. The history of his presenting condition is outlined below.

SIGNS AND SYMPTOMS
- Unable to canter round the field.
- On feet being picked out, difficulty transferring his weight.
- Stiff and straight-legged gait on right hind limb.

VETERINARY DIAGNOSIS
This has been made some years previously – arthritic stifle joint.

PHYSIOTHERAPY TREATMENT
- H-wave therapy to the gluteals, quadriceps, hamstrings, muscle groups.
- H-wave pain relief to the stifle joint.

MANAGEMENT
- Chondroitin sulphate and glucosamine taken orally.
- TTEAM – bodywork and limb circles.

OUTCOME
- Able to mobilise almost instantly.
- Maintenance treatments every four to six weeks.

Teeth

'Cider' is a chestnut eight-year-old mare, and a novice eventer. She was bought from a dealer for a novice to ride. She was a fantastic show jumper.

SIGNS/SYMPTOMS
- Every now and then she exploded, bucking for up to 20 minutes.
- Loss of condition.
- A feeling of something being not quite right.

VETERINARY EVALUATION
- Restricted hind limb gait on the lunge (bilateral), soft and hard.
- Sensitive on palpation of whole of body.
- Solid, locked-up feel of back.

DENTIST:
- Ulcerations.
- Poor occlusion jaw.
- Fractured wolf tooth, lower jaw.

COMPLEMENTARY THERAPIES
- Physiotherapy corrected muscle imbalance.
- Acupuncture relieved back pain.
- Healing as she was stressed and anxious.

TACK
- Saddles were checked for fit and symmetry.
- Bit was assessed relative to her mouth anatomy.
- Noseband, on the advice of the dentist, was just a cavasson, to avoid aggravating the jaw.

OUTCOME (POST TREATMENT)
- No more bucking.
- Back muscles relaxed.
- Improved range of motion.
- Calmer and softer outline.

Tendon Injury

Apple Jack is a nine-year-old gelding, a hunter. He had sustained a superficial flexor tendon (SDFT) injury whilst hunting in deep going the previous season.

SIGNS/SYMPTOMS

On walking down the ramp there was visible swelling on the back of the leg, rapidly filling up the leg. He was lame.

ACTION AND TREATMENT

The vet was called, and he administered NSAID and instructed the owners in cold therapy, compression, bandaging and rest. Seven days after the initial injury the limbs (both forelimbs) were ultrasound scanned. This confirmed a core lesion of the SDFT of the near forelimb.

A course of adequan injections intramuscularly was administered by the vet, and therapy was given from the physiotherapist.

THERAPY

- Massage
- Suppling exercises
- Passive flexions of the fetlock joint
- Ultrasound therapy
- Direct soft tissue manipulations

CLINICAL REASONING FOR THIS THERAPY

- To promote circulation and lymphatic drainage away from the injured site.
- To remove debris and toxins.
- For analgesia/relaxation of the muscles and their general well-being.
- Maintenance of movement and flexibility in other areas not affected by the strain.
- To mobilise the area directly, and to improve nutrition to the area. In order to apply some stress to the area as it enters the remodelling and regeneration phase of healing.
- Ultrasound, to promote collagen orientation and synthesis.
- Longitudinal stretching from day 5.
- Transverse frictions post day 14 (ref. Chap 2 page 20).

MANAGEMENT

- Rubber-floored box, 24ft by 12ft.
- Good outlook and other horses.
- Box-rested for 3 months.
- Hand-walked for 6 weeks.
- Turned out in a small pen, progressing to a larger area.
- After 12 months rest, ridden at walk for 6 weeks. This was alternated with ride and lead.

The outcome of this case is that Apple Jack is now back in work and hunting.

Saddle Problem

'Minty' is a 13.1hh, ten-year-old show-jumping pony. This little chap is the most gutsy, cracking little fellow. I was asked to see him because he was resenting his rider on mounting. He was reported to be stiffer than normal, and to be looking unhappy in himself generally. His performance had deteriorated, and he was no longer going clear jumping.

SIGNS/SYMPTOMS
He was very short-backed in conformation, and had a very wide gait behind at walk and trot. This was apparently longstanding. His saddle appeared to be causing some concern. It was too long for him, and was asymmetric through the panels and at the stirrup bars. The points of the tree were rather mobile and slightly too short. His rider is probably in her last season, and so it was appreciated that she was possibly now too tall for him.

TREATMENT
The veterinarian had thoroughly examined him and passed him fit, to be treated with physiotherapy, with no lameness present. I requested that the saddler attend and refit him with another saddle, which was duly done.

DIAGNOSIS
Due to the deep muscle guarding of the back muscles and altered spinal biomechanics, I opted to treat him using soft tissue manipulation using the 'Ellis' technique. This aimed to correct the sensitivity and muscle guarding. The ultimate effect was to soften and restore pain-free spinal

movement. He received two treatments, with three days' rest after each session, and then made a gradual return to normal work.

OUTCOME
He has made a full, functional recovery, being checked three months later. The wide gait behind remains, but this is common (meaning that it is difficult to cure in chronic problems). It is in part related to his conformation, but as a result means he may have difficulty compensating when he gets other problems.

Musculoskeletal Trauma

'Bob' is a 16.3hh gelding used for riding club activities. He is a TB Irish Sports Horse, and was bought broken in as a four-year-old by his lady owner. He had a five-star vetting, when it was noticed that he had a mild asymmetry of the tuber sacrale; however, there was no sign of lameness.

He is a large horse who managed to fall over in the school within the first couple of weeks of ownership. He was seen immediately by a chartered physiotherapist. He then had a very traumatic accident, in which he galloped across a field, skidded, and landed under a post-and-rail fence where he remained motionless for 20 minutes in this position. He was thoroughly examined by the vet after this.

SIGNS/SYMPTOMS

From this time onwards, he became stiff on the right rein when being schooled. He was assessed by a chartered physiotherapist, who referred him for osteopathy.

TREATMENT

The osteopath employed sustained positional release techniques under sedation. He received three treatments a few weeks apart, with rest in between. He was then brought back into work where he appeared to be back to normal.

Some eight months later he was again uncomfortable on the right rein so he was referred back to his own vet who identified that he was lame on a hard surface on both right and left reins. He was prescribed bute, and rested for five days. He was then re-tested on the hard circle where he appeared to be sound. Two months later he was being inconsistent and occasionally lame on the right rein when

Checking for straightness of the spine

being schooled correctly. He competed in a dressage competition where he was eliminated for being lame.

DIAGNOSIS

He was therefore referred to a specialist hospital for a veterinary work-up. They used ridden tests, nerve blocks, x-rays and gamma scintigraphy. On x-ray he appeared to have a 'flat' pedal bone on the right fore. This was addressed with corrective shoeing by the remedial farrier.

The problem was that this could not be the whole story, and the veterinary opinion at the time considered that the way he was being ridden was contributing to his problem.

SUMMARY

- This horse was showing his symptoms inconsistently, but they were evident when being ridden by an experienced dressage rider and owner.
- He had fallen twice, the latter time severely.
- He had some signs of foot pathology.
- He was not bone scanned in the soft tissue phase, and x-rays do not always identify damage early on, so perhaps diagnosis was not complete.

OUTCOME

Following his discharge, permission was gained to treat him, as he was very restricted in his flexibility, and on palpation of his soft tissues he obviously felt pain. Bob, however, had another fall in the field when he sat down like a dog, and after this he elicited some adverse upper neck tissue sensitivity, and a clinical decision to discontinue manipulative therapy was made. He therefore had acupuncture and healing.

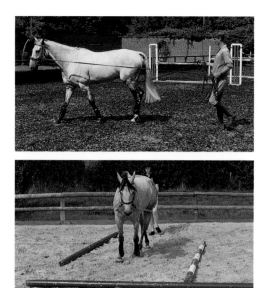

Long-reining, (top) and TTEAM work, as being shown with this horse, was recommended as part of the injury management plan for Bob

MANAGEMENT

Bob fell rather a lot because he was big and fast, and played too much with other horses. The solution was to put him in a field with just one, older horse.

He also had a balance problem. His owner reports that, although very brave, he still has problems co-ordinating his movements – for instance, down a step fence downhill.

Because of the various traumas he has sustained he is almost certain to have caused some damage to his soft tissues, joints, and the proprioceptors and mechanoreceptors. He therefore needed to have some form of training to rehabilitate the neuromotor pathways of his nervous system in order to maximise function.

For example:
- TTEAM
- Groundwork: Parelli and long reining

CONCLUSION

He then went on a very slow rehabilitation programme, building up his exercise to accommodate his particular issues. He is now show jumping and cross-country schooling, some ten months after his last fall.

Thoracic Spine Bone Inflammation

'Max' is a 16.2hh, ten-year-old driving horse; a Gelderlander. For twelve months Max had been a problem when ridden, simply putting on the brakes and refusing to go forwards. His owner is fully trained in Intelligent Horsemanship Skills and uses homoeopathy and healing. She had therefore utilised all these complementary approaches, including physiotherapy. The saddle had been changed, and still the problem continued. They then decided to ride him bareback, but this did not improve the situation. He was, however, relatively okay being driven.

SIGNS/SYMPTOMS

I was asked to see him, and my first concern was that he had not been evaluated by the veterinary surgeon for this problem. He was incredibly sensitive, and actually aggressive on palpation, especially around the lower cervical spine and upper/mid thoracic spine.

DIAGNOSIS

The owner took Max to the vets for use of their specialist facilities. The spine was x-rayed, and it was discovered that he had severe damage to the upper thoracic spine – there was evidence of sclerosis and impingement. This was probably from a fall some time ago.

MANAGEMENT

The prescribed treatment was rest, and after six months a return to driving before ridden exercise. He received healing, and, once the extreme sensitivity had settled, physiotherapy.

TREATMENT

Finally Max was given an intensive course of physiotherapy in his recuperation.

THERAPY	EFFECT
Massage	Analgesia Relieve tension Improve circulation
Mobilisations	To improve range of motion To increase extensibility
Electrotherapy: 　TENS 　LASER 　PSWD	 Analgesia Healing Muscle nutrition
Manual	Cranio-sacral Treatment of pelvic dysfunction

Muscle Injury

Pumpkin, is an 18-year-old driving pony who sustained injury to his biceps femoris muscle when in the field.

SIGNS/SYMPTOMS

A large swelling, which appeared to grow overnight, developed rapidly. It was hot and soft (fluid-filled). The pony was tender around the injury site on palpation.

DIAGNOSIS

The vet evaluated the injury and diagnosed a haematoma, an accumulation of blood within the tissues that clots to form a solid swelling. The vet prescribed NSAIDs, cold packs, and 48 hours box-rest. The owner was anxious to get back into competition, and asked if anything else could be done to enhance the quality of tissue recovery and shorten the time off work. The vet therefore referred them for physiotherapy.

TREATMENT

Day 1: Ice 10 mins every 2 hours.
Day 2: Ice 10 mins x 3 a day.
Day 3:
- Pulsed short-wave diathermy to the injured area.
- Massage to the rest of the limb.
- Heat in the form of hot packs to the surrounding muscle.
- H-wave (muscle stimulation) and pain relief.

Day 5: Start longitudinal stretches, direct pressure techniques.

Day 14: Deep transverse frictions.

Days 5–14 Exercise:
- After 48 hours he was hand-walked for 10 minutes, three times a day.
- By day 5 he was being long-reined for 20 minutes, twice a day.
- By day 14 he was trotting and walking up to forty minutes on long reins.
- By day 21 he had started driving, on walking exercise initially, slowly building up over a period of three weeks.

MANAGEMENT

This pony made a good recovery, but his owner will continue to stretch his hamstrings for the rest of his life.

1 Day 5–Day 21 is very important for collagen orientation and healing. The area must be tensioned to encourage a functional outcome and to maximise tensile strength.

2 Stretches: Exercise for 10 minutes to warm up the area, and then perform a hamstring stretch (ref. *The Injury Free Horse*). Hold at the end of the range for 15 secs, and repeat twice.

> **KEY POINT:** Massage can be used to warm up the area as an alternative to exercise.

Practical
Treatment

We know that to rely on single treatments to 'cure all' and maintain function in our own bodies is unreasonable, so it comes as no surprise to find that the horse is no different. The re-education of movement patterns and the correction and relearning of normal posture, the strengthening of weak muscles and relaxation of over-active ones, all play an ongoing part in restoring health and the ability to perform. We therefore have to apply a variety of techniques to make this happen. As we cannot ask the horse verbally improve his posture or movement it is up to us to position him correctly and produce the effect either locally, at muscle, joint or skin level, or by creating an effect on the central nervous system that leads to the required change in movement or local muscle tone.

Palpatory Assessment

With reference to the accompanying diagram, structures are listed from bottom to top, front to back, and superficial to deep. The muscles in bold print are the ones most likely to be felt.

Areas of muscle palpation

1 Splenius, brachiocephalicus, semispinalis capitis/complexus, longissimus capitis, **obliquus capitis crainialis**, rectus capitis dorsalis major and minor, nuchal ligament.
2 Splenius, **brachiocephalicus**, semispinalis/complexus, **longissimus capitis & atlantis, obliquus capitis caudalis**, rectus capitis dorsalis minor, nuchal ligament.
3 **Trapezius**, rhomboideus, splenius, semispinalis/complexus, nuchal ligament.
4 **Splenius, serratus ventralis cervicalis**, trapezius, cranial deep pectoral, longsissimus capitis and atlantis, semispinalis/complexus.
5 **Brachiocephalicus**, omotransversus, iliocostalis (cervical), intertransversarii, multifidus, rectus capitis ventralis.
6 Sternocephalicus, sternohyoid/thyroid.
7 Trapezius, **cranial deep pectoral, serratus ventralis cervicalis**, longsissimus capitis and atlantis, iliocostalis (cervical), intertransversarii, multifidus, omotransversus.
8 **Supraspinatus**.
9 **Infraspinatus**.
10 **Superficial pectorals, deep pectorals**.
11 Teres minor, **long head of triceps, deltoid**.
12 **Serratus ventralis thoracis**, intercostals, caudal deep pectoral, external oblique.

13 **Trapezius**, rhomboideus, semispinalis/complexus.
14 **Longissimus (thoracic and lumbar), middle gluteal (gluteal tongue)**, spinalis, multifidus.
15 **Iliocostalis (thoracic and lumbar)**, middle gluteal, serratus dorsalis (cranial and caudal).
16 **Latissimus dorsi**, intercostals.
17 **Caudal deep pectoral, rectus abdominis**.
18 Superficial gluteal, middle gluteal, deep gluteal, **biceps femoris, semitendinosus**.
19 **Tensor fascia lata**, internal oblique, iliacus.
20 **TFL, quadriceps (rectus femoris and vastus lateralis)**, gluteal tendons.
21 **Biceps femoris, semitendinosus, + semimembranosus** medially.
22 **Gracilis, adductor** and semimembranosus.
23a **Gastrocnemius**, soleus, digital flexors.
23 **Flexors of hock and digital extensors**.
24a **Carpodigital flexors**.
24 **Biceps, brachialis, carpodigital extensors**.
25 **Sacrocaudalis dorsalis and ventralis, intertransversarii**.

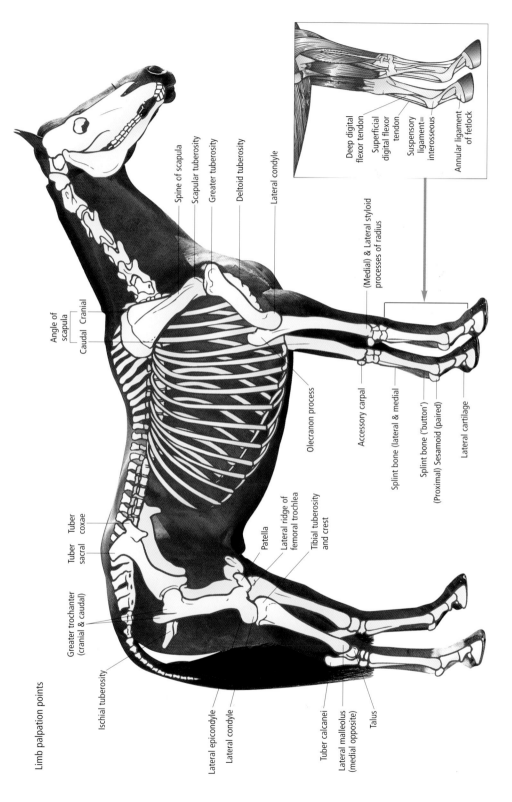

Limb palpation points

Deep digital flexor tendon

Superficial digital flexor tendon

Suspensory ligament= interosseous

Annular ligament of fetlock

Spine of scapula

Scapular tuberosity

Greater tuberosity

Deltoid tuberosity

Lateral condyle

(Medial) & Lateral styloid proceses of radius

Angle of scapula

Caudal Cranial

Olecranon process

Accessory carpal

Splint bone (lateral & medial)

Splint bone ('button')

(Proximal) Sesamoid (paired)

Lateral cartilage

Tuber coxae

Tuber sacral

Greater trochanter (cranial & caudal)

Ischial tuberosity

Patella

Lateral ridge of femoral trochlea

Tibial tuberosity and crest

Lateral epicondyle

Lateral condyle

Tuber calcanei

Lateral malleolus (medial opposite)

Talus

145

Stress points

1 Rectus capitus lateralis
2 Multifidus cervicus
3 Brachiocephalicus
4 Triceps
5 Posterior pectoral
6 Gluteals
7 Gluteals
8 Iliacus
9 Biceps femoris

Technique

Apply compression using either a thumb, fingers or clenched fist. Apply 10 seconds light pressure and 10 seconds medium pressure.

In the 7/8/9 area apply a further 15 seconds of deep pressure

Practical Treatments

ABDOMINAL AND SPINAL REFLEXES

If the horse is restricted in the abdominal lift reflex, then practising it will help to get it going again. This response (belly lift) is essential for normal ridden exercise, because without it the horse will not be able to lift the forehand and work from behind.

SUITABLE CANDIDATES FOR ABDOMINAL REFLEX TRAINING EXERCISE

- Older horses with sway backs obviously have weak abdominals.
- Resting or post-rested horse.
- Post injury, such as a fall.
- Horses with painful feet or hocks. They change their posture to save themselves, and as a consequence, become 'flabby' around the middle.
- Spinal stiffness.

This horse has a conformational sway back which is desirable in its breed but may produce problems

Method 1

First of all, be sure to have a handler at the horse's head, to prevent a sudden response or pull back. Always take care, and in particular be aware of the horse's mood and wary of the hind limbs in case it suddenly kicks out at you.

1 Place your hands together in a cupped, 'paw' position.
2 Face the horse and position the hands to the underside of the belly, as far across to the opposite side as you can.
3 With a drawing movement, quickly caress towards you…
4 …lifting the stomach upwards as you come.
5 Focus the eyes on the withers' summit so you can see the effect. Hold for three seconds, and repeat twice.
6 To take this exercise a stage further, try holding the lift for up to ten seconds.

Reflex stimulation points

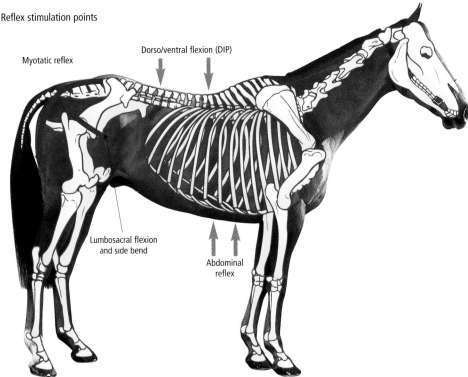

Myotatic reflex

Dorso/ventral flexion (DIP)

Lumbosacral flexion
and side bend

Abdominal
reflex

Method 2

1 Use a long towel and stand on a safe object at the side of the horse. Place the towel under the belly and up towards the withers to your hands.

2 Lift the towel upwards to encourage lift.

3 Hold for three seconds and relax, repeat twice.

4 Take this exercise a stage further by increasing the hold time to ten seconds.

Talk to your vet if the horse severely resents this exercise, even after a few attempts. It may be just your technique that's aggravating him, or he could have spinal pain.

Method 3

• Using a blunt object, for example a hoofpick, briskly stimulate the horse's tummy, starting from the midline behind the elbows, and moving briskly towards the mid-belly.

Response: The back will lift up and the head will drop.

MYOTATIC REFLEX

Lumbosacral Flexion

The aim of this exercise is to encourage spinal flexion and to open all the joints of the back. It also stretches the topline musculature.

Lumbosacral flexion and lateral movement

Method 1

• A brisk finger-pad pressure from the tuber sacrale, down the side of the buttock, to the junction with the top of the leg.

Response: The horse will curl and tuck the bottom under.

Method 2

• Apply brisk finger-tip pressure from the tuber coxae, across and up to the topline.

Response: The horse should curl the hindquarters and flex the back away from you.

> **CAUTION:** This is a potentially high risk exercise to yourself, so always protect yourself in your positioning, and ask an expert to teach you initially.

Useful Addresses/Websites

To find a CST practitioner, look at the International Association of Healthcare Practitioners (IAHP) Directory website www.iahp.com for a list of professionals.
www.upledger.com
www.natural-animal-health.co.uk
www.taranet.co.uk/trainingeducation.htm

Owner courses
- ITEC Diploma in Equine Sports Massage (UK)
- Equinology (UK and USA).
- Equissage www.equissage.com
- Amanda Sutton (Animal physiotherapy education) www.animaltherapy.co.uk

Other useful contacts
- emrt@ozemail.com.au (worldwide)
- emrt@ozemailuk.co.uk
- www.emrt.eques.com.au
- American Physical Therapy Association (APTA) www.apta.org
- Association of Chartered Physiotherapists in Animal Therapy (ACPAT) *www.acpat.clara.net*
- Canadian Horse and Animal Physiotherapy Association (CHAP) Tel. 403/932 – 4909
- Lincoln Stable Mirror (see p117) www.jacksonarenas.com Tel/Fax. 01647 24022

Further Reading

Back, Willem, Clayton, Hilary and Sanders, W. B. *Equine Locomotion* ISBN 0-7020-2483-X.
Coates, Margrit. *Healing for Horses. The Essential Guide to Using Hands-On Healing Energy with Horses.* Sterling Publications ISBN 0-806-98963-7
Clayton, Hilary M. *Conditioning Sports Horses* Sport Horse Publications ISBN 0-9695-720-0-X.
Dale, Ron and Bob Myler *A Whole Bit Better.*

Equine Injury, Therapy and Rehabilitation Blackwell Science ISBN 0-632-03608-7.
Tellington-Jones, Linda, *Getting in Touch with Horses* Kenilworth Press ISBN 1-872082-74-2.
Williams, Gail and Deacon, Martin *No Foot, No Horse* Kenilworth Press Limited ISBN 1-72119-48-4.
Wyche, Sarah *Understanding the Horse's Back* Crowood Press Limited ISBN 1-861261-14-4.

PICTURE ACKNOWLEDGEMENTS
All photographs from the author's collection except the following:
Fiona Scott-Maxwell: p3
Ian Hemingway: pp 6, 129, 130, 131, 134
Kit Houghton: pp 7(top), 37, 45, 106, 109, 110(top), 112, 113, 128, 147
Bob Langrish: p 7(btm)
Colin Vogel: pp 16, 33, 34, 39, 41, 56, 108, 111
David & Charles: pp 23, 31(btm), 45, 55, 123, 133, 139, 143(Bob Langrish); 28, 32, 53(Andrew Perkins); 93, 94, 115, 116(top), 121, 126(SusanMcBane); 66(Matthew Roberts); 108(Bob Atkins)
Helen Revington: pp 43, 60
Tony Pavord: pp 46, 47, 49, 87
Equissage: p 82

Margrit Coates: pp 87, 102, 103
Equine Bowen (Beth Darrall): p 92
Sue Devereaux: pp 95, 97
ACPAT: p 101
Shona Wallis: p 116(btm)
Jackson Arenas: p 117
Your Horse magazine: p 127
"Les Garennes": p 142

All artworks by Ethan Danielson except the following:
Amanda Sutton: pp 14, 19, 20, 51
David & Charles: pp 37, 39, 125(Maggie Raynor); 40, 111, 145, 148(Paul Bale), 46, 50, 65(Chartwell Illustrators)
Eva Melhuish: p 131(top)

Index

152